WH… IAN?

DAN DIDIO SVP-EXECUTIVE EDITOR **MATT IDELSON** EDITOR-ORIGINAL SERIES
NACHIE CASTRO ASSOCIATE EDITOR-ORIGINAL SERIES
WIL MOSS ASSISTANT EDITOR-ORIGINAL SERIES
GEORG BREWER VP-DESIGN & DC DIRECT CREATIVE
BOB HARRAS GROUP EDITOR-COLLECTED EDITIONS
BOB JOY EDITOR **ROBBIN BROSTERMAN** DESIGN DIRECTOR-BOOKS

DC COMICS
PAUL LEVITZ PRESIDENT & PUBLISHER **RICHARD BRUNING** SVP-CREATIVE DIRECTOR
PATRICK CALDON EVP-FINANCE & OPERATIONS **AMY GENKINS** SVP-BUSINESS & LEGAL AFFAIRS
JIM LEE EDITORIAL DIRECTOR-WILDSTORM **GREGORY NOVECK** SVP-CREATIVE AFFAIRS
STEVE ROTTERDAM SVP-SALES & MARKETING **CHERYL RUBIN** SVP-BRAND MANAGEMENT

Cover by Joshua Middleton. Publication design by Robbie Biederman.

SUPERGIRL: WHO IS SUPERWOMAN?
Published by DC Comics.

DC Comics, 1700 Broadway, New York, NY 10019
A Warner Bros. Entertainment Company
Printed by World Color Press, Inc,
St-Romuald, QC, Canada 10/14/09. First Printing.
ISBN: 978-1-4012-2507-0

SUSTAINABLE FORESTRY INITIATIVE
Certified Fiber Sourcing
www.sfiprogram.org
Fiber used in this product line meets the sourcing requirements of the SFI program. www.sfiprogram.org PWC-SFICOC-260

SUPERGIRL

WHO IS SUPERWOMAN?

STERLING GATES
WRITER

JAMAL IGLE
WITH:
FERNANDO DAGNINO
TALENT CALDWELL
MATTHEW CLARK
PENCILLERS

KEITH CHAMPAGNE
WITH:
JON SIBAL
TALENT CALDWELL
RAÚL FERNANDEZ
MATTHEW CLARK
INKERS

NEI RUFFINO
WITH:
TOM CHU
COLORISTS

JARED K. FLETCHER
WITH:
ROB LEIGH
LETTERERS

JOSHUA MIDDLETON
ORIGINAL SERIES COVERS

INTRODUCTION BY
HELEN SLATER

INTRODUCTION

by **HELEN SLATER**

When I read the new comic for Supergirl, I was struck by the drama of a teenage girl unable to harness her gift in a way that helped the world. In fact, her superpowers cause more harm than good. It is heartbreaking that Kara wants to do right with her powers but is unable to, or not yet ready to fully understand them. Is this just a comic book we are reading or is it actually a modern myth, quietly offering insight about the teenage experience?

Although Supergirl is Kryptonian, there is a way in which we can recognize all American teenagers with this myth. Teenagers are powerful because their energy can be so raw and spectacular. They are discovering, claiming and celebrating their innate gifts, but do not yet have the refinement to negotiate with the outside world.

We all identify with the challenges of having to relate socially to the world around us. We are obligated in our society to be civil and obey the law. We must, to a certain degree, live “within the lines.” But as teenagers, we have not fully acquired those skills. Guided by the urge to help, we swoop into places we do not belong and this can get us into trouble. The rite of passage of growing out of our awkward, teenage “duckling” experience into beautiful, elegant swans is both painful and challenging.

So how, as humans, do we do it? With the guidance of friends, parents and teachers, we eventually find some kind of balance between our inner creative gifts and the outside world. And, of course, by falling down again and again until our knocks and scrapes awaken the sleepy intuitive voice that hums eternal in each of us.

Supergirl has Superman, Batman, Wonder Woman and Lana Lang to illuminate the path to adulthood. When a teenager is given too much power, it is almost to be expected that they will not be able to handle it. We have examples of this in young celebrities and ordinary kids alike, who are feeling out of control because of too much freedom. What should be a time of metamorphosis, as the caterpillar becomes the butterfly, can be corrupted by unlimited choices.

In the end, Supergirl gets burned by trying to do too much too soon and not taking the appropriate time to simmer and stew the brew of her internal light. One of the wonderful things about this comic book series is how freewheeling and bombastic Supergirl’s teenage life is. It makes for great reading. And I believe it also taps into something recognizable to all of us.

HELEN SLATER *made her big-screen debut playing the title role of Supergirl in 1984. Since then the actress has made numerous television, movie and theater appearances. Helen has also released two albums of original music since 2003. Currently, she can be seen in a recurring role as Clark Kent's Kryptonian mother, Lara, on the TV series Smallville.*

WHY THE WORLD DOES NOT NEED A SUPER*GIRL*

By CAT GRANT

Supergirl is not Superman. From the very beginning, her actions have seemed hollow and forced, proving her not only unworthy of the legacy of Superman's symbol, but also unworthy to serve as the protector of Metropolis. Supergirl has been the source

"I think Supergirl thought being the hero would be an easy job, but it's not. Far from it," says Travis DuBarry, the newly appointed Captain of the Science Police. "Supergirl actually showed up to our fight with Atlas last week [see sidebar] and watched him

WHY THE WORLD DOESN'T NEED SUPERGIRL

JAMAL IGLE PENCILS
KEITH CHAMPAGNE INKS

YESTERDAY.
AILY PLANET
DAILY PLANET
"A Great Metropolitan Newspaper"
75¢
y Edition
HY THE WORLD DOESN'T NEED SUPERGIRL
YOU'RE NOT SERIOUSLY GOING TO RUN THAT, ARE YOU, MR. WHITE?
Photo by JAM
GRANT
nment & Arts
orrespondent
Perry-- Pls. OK THIS BEFORE 10am. Jamal
THIS WAS THE ONLY SALVAGEABLE PHOTO? DON'T WE HAVE A STOCK SHOT?

WHY WOULDN'T I RUN IT, KENT?
AN EXPOSÉ ON THE IRRESPONSIBILITY OF ONE OF THE CITY'S BIGGEST HEROES? IT'S A SOLID STORY!
BESIDES, CAT PREEMPTIVELY WINED AND DINED THE PUBLISHERS LAST WEEK, AND NOW THEY WANT TO SEE THIS DEFAMATION ON THE STANDS JUST AS MUCH AS SHE DOES.
PERRY, SUPERGIRL DOES A LOT OF GOOD FOR THIS CITY. SHE'S A HERO. IF SHE SEES THIS...
CHIEF, COULDN'T YOU RUN IT SOMEWHERE ELSE? I MEAN, WOULDN'T THIS ARTICLE BE MORE SUITED FOR THE OPINION PAGE?
OPINION PAGE?
YOU WANT TO BURY ME BETWEEN TROUPE'S POLITICAL COLUMN AND "DEAR ABBY"?
OLSEN AND I WERE NEARLY KILLED FOR THAT STORY. IT'S FRONT PAGE OR NOTHING.
LANA LANG FOR YOU ON LINE ONE, MR. WHITE.
TELL HER I'LL CALL HER BACK, GRACE.
'MORNING, CAT. KENT AND LANE AND I WERE JUST DISCUSSING YOUR ARTICLE.
YOUR LIBEL, HE MEANS.
LIBEL, LOIS? SUPERGIRL IS KRYPTONIAN, MAKING HER THE MOST POWERFUL TEENAGER ON THE PLANET.
SHE'S SO POWERFUL SHE CAN'T BE BOTHERED TO WORRY ABOUT THE SAFETY OF ANYONE SHE'S TRYING TO "SAVE."
PEOPLE LIKE THE PHOTOGRAPHER SHE SHOVES TO THE GROUND--
--OR THE PERSON THAT PHOTOGRAPHER LANDS ON.

MS. GRANT, YOU KNOW SUPERGIRL WAS TRYING TO SAVE US FROM BEING HIT BY FALLING DEBRIS! IT WAS AN ACCIDENT!
AN ACCIDENT THAT COST YOU A CAMERA, JAMES.
THAT'S OKAY-- SUPERMAN DOES IT TO ME ALL THE TIME.
SEPTEM
LOOK, WHEN THE AMAZONS ATTACKED WASHINGTON, SUPERGIRL HELPED BRING DOWN AIR FORCE ONE, AN "ACCIDENT" THAT PUT TWENTY-SIX PEOPLE IN THE HOSPITAL AND NEARLY KILLED THE PRESIDENT.
SHE BROKE A MAN'S ARM IN THREE DIFFERENT PLACES PULLING HIM OUT OF A BUILDING AT SUPER-SPEED WHILE FIGHTING REACTRON LAST MONTH.
SCIENCE POLICE CAPTAIN DuBARRY TOLD ME SHE POPPED UP WHILE THEY WERE FIGHTING ATLAS, SAW THEM LOSING, THEN FLEW AWAY.
AND DON'T EVEN GET ME STARTED ON POOR THOMAS KENKEL PRICE.
SHE PROMISED THAT BOY SHE'D CURE HIS TERMINAL BRAIN TUMOR. HIS PARENTS ARE STILL TRYING TO FIGURE OUT WHOM THEY CAN SUE FOR EMOTIONAL DURESS.
SHE'S AVOIDING TAKING BLAME. LIKE ANY TEENAGER WHO KNOWS THEY'RE IN TROUBLE.
SUPERGIRL MIGHT NOT HAVE THE BEST AVERAGE, CAT, BUT THAT DOESN'T MEAN YOU SHOULD CALL FOR HER RESIGNATION.
OH, I'M NOT ASKING HER TO RESIGN, CLARK.
Tsk. THAT SKIRT'S INDECENT.
I JUST WANT HER FAR FROM METROPOLIS--
--AND FAR AWAY FROM ME.
DAILY PLANET
WHY THE WORLD DOESN'T NEED SUPERGIRL

TODAY.
TEN MINUTES AGO, THE SILVER BANSHEE WALKED INTO AN OCCULT BOOKSTORE IN GOTHAM AND SCREAMED SO LOUD, IT SHATTERED EARDRUMS AND WINDOWS FOR HALF A MILE.
I FLEW IN, KNOCKED HER OUT, AND THEN HEADED FOR STRYKER'S ISLAND, WHERE THEY CAN DEAL WITH PEOPLE LIKE HER.
WONDER GIRL CALLS IT THE "JAB-AND-GRAB."
THE BANSHEE CAME TO EN ROUT AND STARTED WAILING.
IT'S REALLY HARD TO KEEP YOUR EQUILIBRIUM IN THE AIR WITH SOMEONE SCREAMING A BILLION DECIBELS IN YOUR FACE.
I THINK SHE BURST MY LEF EARDRUM.
SHUT UP, YOU ANNOYING
YEAH, EARDRUM'S OUT. STUPID SUPER-HEARING.
I'M
SUPERGIRL
THIS IS MY LIFE.

CHOOOOMPH
D-DID YOU SEE THAT?
WHAT *WAS* IT?
AIM FOR THE STARS
I THINK THAT WAS SUPERMAN!
BUT WHAT WAS HE *FIGHTING?*

S-SUPERMAN--?

ARE YOU--?

HEY, GIMME A HAND OVER HERE! I THINK SUPERMAN'S--

SSSSSSSSSS
KAL-EL TOLD ME...
THE BANSHEE IS SUPERNATURAL IN NATURE, KARA--
"--AND SHE'S THE WORST KIND OF CRIMINAL. A SPREE KILLER.
"THERE'S NEITHER RHYME NOR REASON WHEN SHE KILLS.
"YOU DO HAVE AN ADVANTAGE GOING UP AGAINST HER, THOUGH.
"SHE CAN SCREAM AT YOU ALL SHE LIKES, BUT THE ONLY WAY HER WAIL CAN KILL IS IF YOU HEAR HER SCREAM YOUR TRUE NAME."
GUH--!
FAIR--
NO!
"AND AS LONG AS YOU DON'T TELL HER YOU'RE KARA ZOR-EL--"

"--YOU'LL BE SAFE AS HOUSES."
STAYRIGHT THEREYOU'LLBE SAFESORRY!
WHAT THE--?
WHAT?
HEY, WATCH IT!
HOW SAFE IS A HOUSE, ANYWAY?
--CHIILLDDDEEEEEEEE!
SSSSSS
YO! BANSHEE!

SKRAAAANNSH
GOAL!
OR WHATEVER THEY SAY IN BASEBALL.
HEY, SUPERGIRL!
SKRSSSH
WHY'D YOU HAVETA CRASH HERE?! YOU RUINED OUR GAME!
I PAID SIX HUNDRED BUCKS FOR THESE SEATS!
SUPERMAN WOULDN'TA TRASHED THE FIELD LIKE THAT!
YEAH!
IT WAS A TIE GAME! A TIE!
WHAT'RE WE GONNA DO NOW?

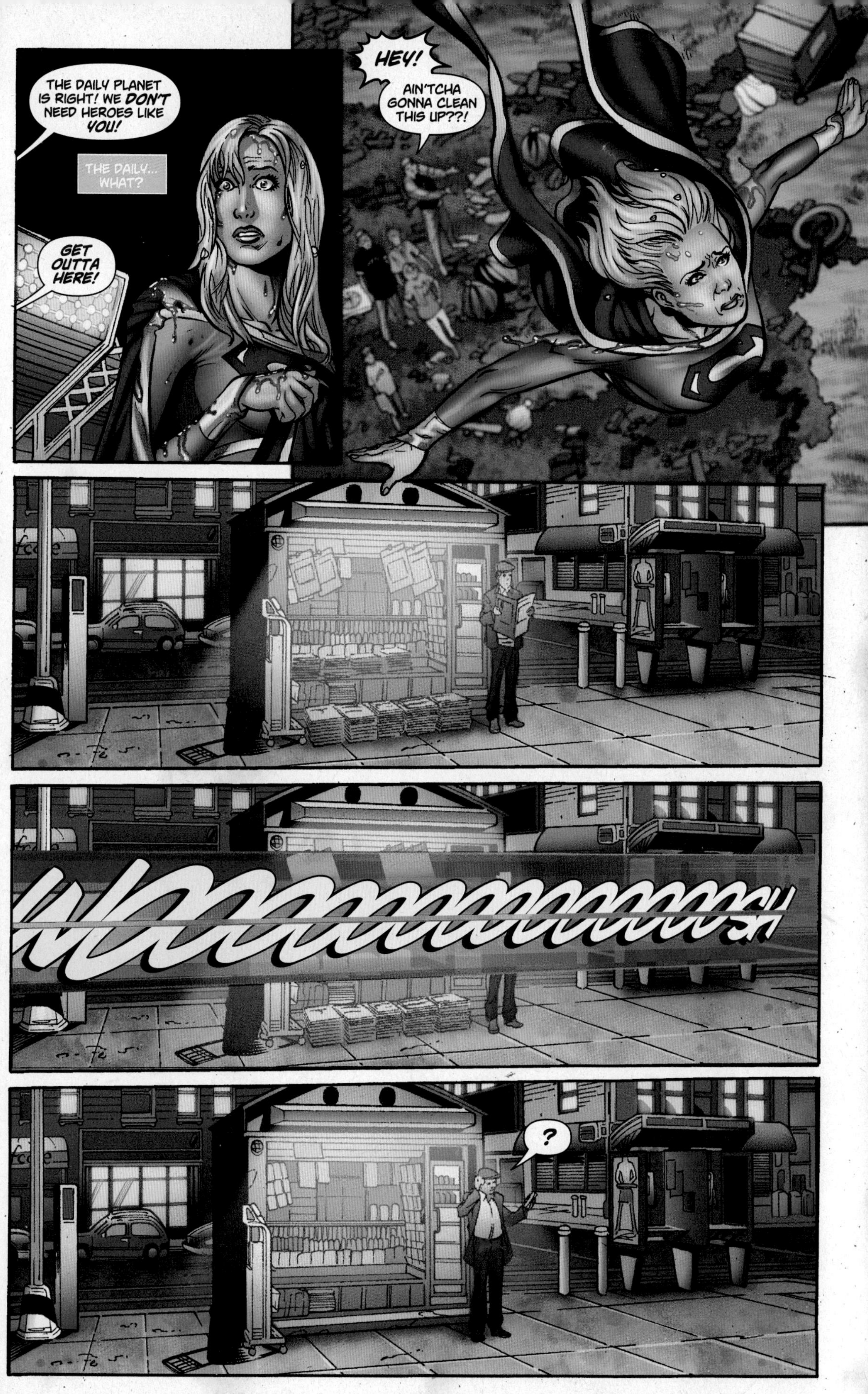
THE DAILY PLANET IS RIGHT! WE DON'T NEED HEROES LIKE YOU!
THE DAILY... WHAT?
GET OUTTA HERE!
HEY!
AIN'TCHA GONNA CLEAN THIS UP??!
WOOOOOOOOOOOOSH
?

DAILY PLANET
WHY THE WORLD DOESN'T NEED SUPERGIRL
KARA, I'M SORRY.
HOW COULD YOU?

HOW COULD YOU LET THEM RUN SOMETHING LIKE THIS, KAL? HOW COULD YOU LET THIS...THIS WOMAN TALK ABOUT ME LIKE THIS?
KARA, SHE--
DO YOU THINK SHE'S RIGHT?
DAILY PLANET
WHY THE WORLD DOESN'T NEED SUPERGIRL
WHAT?
IS SHE RIGHT, KAL?
AM I "A TARTED-UP TEENAGER IN A SHORT SKIRT AND CAPE WITH SOMETHING TO PROVE"?
AM I "NOT WORTHY OF THE LEGACY OF SUPERMAN"?
I THINK YOU'RE MORE THAN WORTHY.
YOU SAY THAT, BUT...
...IT'S HARD FOR ME TO PROVE MY WORTH IF YOU HAVE TO BAIL ME OUT EVERY TIME I GET INTO TROUBLE, KAL.

KARA, THE PEOPLE DOWN THERE EXPECT US TO BE PERFECT. INFALLIBLE. TO ALWAYS MAKE THE RIGHT DECISIONS.
BUT WE CAN'T ALWAYS DO THAT. AND SOMETIMES, CERTAIN PEOPLE LIKE TO POINT IT OUT IN THE WORST WAY POSSIBLE.
EVERYONE MAKES MISTAKES. EVERYONE. YOU CAN'T LET THEM GET TO YOU.
BUT KAL, EVEN WHEN I TRY TO DO EVERYTHING RIGHT, PEOPLE STILL GET HURT. THEY STILL GET MAD.
YOU'RE LEARNING. IT'S IMPOSSIBLE TO GET EVERYTHING RIGHT.
AND CAT GRANT'S WRONG.
THE WORLD NEEDS HEROES LIKE US.
FOR A WORLD THAT NEEDS US, THEY SURE CAN BE JERKS ABOUT IT.
KARA, I WASN'T GOING TO SUGGEST THIS, BUT...
...MAYBE IT'S TIME YOU TRIED SOMETHING DIFFERENT.

OU THINK
SHOULD
STOP--?
NO.
BUT KARA, YOU SPEND SO MUCH TIME TRYING TO SAVE EVERYONE ELSE, TO BE THE HERO THAT EVERYONE EXPECTS YOU TO BE, YOU DON'T GET A CHANCE TO RELAX.
YOU'RE SUPERGIRL TWENTY-FOUR HOURS A DAY, AND I THINK IT'S STARTING TO HURT MORE THAN HELP.
IF THE WORLD DOESN'T NEED YOU ALL THE TIME--
--MAYBE YOU SHOULD TRY JUST BEING A PART OF THE WORLD. IT'S EASY.
AND YOUR FIRST STEP TOWARDS MAKING A SECRET IDENTITY?
PICK OUT A NEW NAME FOR YOURSELF. YOUR HUMAN NAME.
OKAY. IF YOU THINK IT CAN HELP, I'LL DO IT.
THE CITY IS REALLY PRETTY IN THE MORNING.
YES, IT IS.
CAT GRANT IS A TOTAL
YES, SHE IS.

FO, WHAF YUR NAME GUNNA BE?
UM, GROSS.
THORRY.
I DON'T KNOW, EDDIE. I HAVEN'T DECIDED ON MY NAME YET.
I WAS HOPING BATMAN WOULD SET ME UP WHEN I DO. BIRTH CERTIFICATE, DIPLOMA, THE WORKS.
I WENT BY THE CAVE, BUT EVERYTHING WAS... WELL, TRASHED.
IS BATMAN OKAY, ROBIN?
FOLLOW ME.
DO THEY ALL GET THEIR OWN CAVES?
BATMAN'S... OFF THE GRID, KARA, AND I DON'T SET UP IDENTITIES FOR PEOPLE.
TALK TO ORACLE. THOUGH I THINK SUPERMAN ALREADY PUT HER ON IT THIS MORNING.
HE WHAT?
I KNOW YOU'RE STILL NOT SURE WHAT YOUR NEW I.D. WILL BE, KARA, BUT IF IT HELPS AT ALL--
--THESE WERE CONNER'S.
I THINK HE'D BE GLAD SOMEONE IN HIS FAMILY WAS GETTING TO USE THEM.

...AND SINCE NOLAN CLAY RETIRED, THE BUSINESS SECTION'S BEEN ADRIFT. RUDDERLESS.
I COULD USE SOMEONE WITH YOUR KIND OF CORPORATE EXPERIENCE TO STEER THAT SHIP--
--LANA.
PERRY, I KNOW WHAT YOU WANT M TO SAY, BUT I'M N COMING BACK TO METROPOLIS.
I SACRIFICED EVERYTHING I HAD--
--AND ALL LEXCORP DID WAS USE ME UP AND THROW ME TO THE STREET.
SO I'M REALLY SORRY, PERRY, BUT MY ANSWER IS STILL NO. I'M STAYING IN SMALLVILLE.
PLEASE DON'T CALL ME AGAIN.
CLICK
LEXCORP
Shaping your future, today!

RRAAARRKK!
YOU TALKED WITH THE LEAGUE ALREADY?
NNG.
THEY ALL AGREED I SHOULD WEAR A MASK.
SAID IT MAKES KEEPING THE SECRET IDENTITY EASIER.
HOLD STILL, BUCKBEAK!
FWOOSH
HEY! CUT IT OUT!
HWOOSHING
HHH HHH
THANK YOU FOR THE HELP, KARA.
WHILE I'VE NEVER BEEN ONE TO WEAR A MASK--

--I DO THINK HAVING ANOTHER IDENTITY MAKES THINGS EASIER SOMETIMES.
HAVING A CIVILIAN NAME NOT ONLY EMPOWERS YOU, IT CAN ALSO MAKE YOU VULNERABLE.
IF YOU MAKE FRIENDS WITH YOUR NEW NAME, HAVE... RELATIONSHIPS WITH PEOPLE WHO AREN'T LIKE US--
--YOUR ENEMIES CAN STRIKE OUT AT THEM AS THEY WOULD AT YOU.
RRRAAWK!
BUT THINK ON THIS--WHEN THE JUSTICE LEAGUE TELLS YOU TO PUT ON A MASK--
--THEY MIGHT NOT MEAN WEAR ONE WHILE YOU'RE IN COSTUME.
SOUNDS... COMPLEX.
HIDING ONE'S INNER NATURE WITH A NORMAL EXTERIOR ISN'T SIMPLE.
SOME ARE MORE SUCCESSFUL WITH IT THAN OTHERS. CLARK AND BRUCE ARE AMONG THE BEST.
JUST REMEMBER TO BE CAREFUL, KARA. IN THE WRONG HANDS--

"--THE NAME YOU CHOOSE WILL BE DANGEROUS."
U.S. MAIL
KENT
SHE'S GOT SOME HARD CHOICES IN FRONT OF HER.
SHE BARELY SAID ANYTHING AT DINNER.
YOU HEARD CLARK. GIRL'S HIT A BAD PATCH. STILL, I'M NOT SURE WE'VE DONE ENOUGH TO HELP HER.
I DOUBT SHE'LL LISTEN TO A COUPLE OF OLD FOLKS LIKE US, ANYWAY--
"--SO I CALLED IN FOR SOME BACKUP."
HEY, SUPERGIRL...
...WHY SO GLUM?

THEY FIRED YOU FOR TRYING TO SAVE KAL'S LIFE?
MY CONTRACT SAID I'D NEVER USE LEXCORP TO HELP SUPERMAN. I DID, SO HERE I AM. HIDING OUT AT MY MOM'S HOUSE IN SMALLVILLE.
WHAT'RE YOU GONNA DO NOW?
I DON'T KNOW. THE PLANET OFFERED ME A JOB--
SO NOT MY FAVORITE NEWS SOURCE RIGHT NOW.
YEAH, I SAW THE ARTICLE.
DON'T WORRY ABOUT CAT. SHE'D RATHER CRUCIFY SOMEONE ON THE FRONT PAGE THAN REPORT ACTUAL NEWS.
LANA, CAN I ASK YOU SOMETHING?
GO FOR IT.
WHEN I FIRST SAW THAT ARTICLE, ALL I COULD THINK WAS, "ARE THEY RIGHT? DOES THE WORLD NEED ME?"
KAL'S SOLUTION WAS TO MAKE UP A NEW NAME AND HIDE FROM MY PROBLEMS.
EVERYONE I TALKED TO AGREED WITH HIM. EVEN WONDER WOMAN.
BUT IF THE WORLD DOESN'T NEED SUPERGIRL, IF I WOULD BE BETTER OFF AS SOMEONE ELSE--
--SHOULD I JUST HOLE UP SOMEWHERE UNTIL I CAN GET A BETTER HANDLE ON BEING ME?

KARA, CLARK DOESN'T ALWAYS HAVE THE BEST ADVICE.
DON'T GIVE UP YOUR ENTIRE LIFE BECAUSE YOU MADE SOME RASH DECISIONS AND GOT ON A REPORTER'S BAD SIDE.
YOU CAN'T HIDE OR STOP BEING YOU JUST BECAUSE SOMEONE DECIDES THEY DON'T...LIKE...
...YOU...
LANA?
Y'KNOW, I THINK WE HAVE THE EXACT SAME PROBLEM.
WE DON'T WANT TO DISAPPOINT ANY OF THE PEOPLE WHO LOVE US, WHO WANNA PULL US OUT OF THE STATE WE'RE IN--
--BUT WE'RE NOT SURE WE HAVE THE STRENGTH TO GET BACK ON OUR FEET ALONE.
HOW STRONG ARE YOU, KARA?
I'M SUPERGIRL. STRONGEST GIRL ON THE PLANET.
THOUGHT SO.
I'VE GOT AN IDEA...

IN THE END, LANA KNEW EXACTLY WHAT TO DO.
OLSEN!
WE'RE NOT PAYING YOU TO TAKE PICTURES OF GARBAGE TRUCKS ON BASEBALL FIELDS!
NAMES CAN MAKE YOU VULNERABLE.
IF I ASK YOU FOR PRIZE-WINNING SHOTS OF SUPERGIRL, YOU BRING ME PRIZE-WINNING SHOTS OF SUPERGIRL!
HEY, WHO LEFT--?
BUT THEY CAN ALSO BE A GREAT SOURCE OF STRENGTH.
YOU GOT IT, CHIEF!
Cat--
--Don't call me if you ever get stuck in a tree.
S-Girl
IT'S NOT IMPORTANT THAT THE WORLD ALWAYS NEEDS ME, OR THAT I ALWAYS LIVE UP TO SUPERMAN'S NAME.
'MORNING, GUYS.
WHAT'S IMPORTANT IS NOT HIDING FROM MY PROBLEMS AND TRUSTING THAT I'LL FIND MY PLACE IN THE WORLD--
--THEN MAKING SURE I HAVE MY FAMILY WHEN I GET THERE.
HEY, HAVE YOU TWO EVER MET MY NIECE?

I'D LIKE TO INTRODUCE MS. LINDA LANG.
HI. VERY NICE TO MEET YOU.
Meteors
DAILY PLANET
LANG, LANA
DAILY PLANET
VISITOR

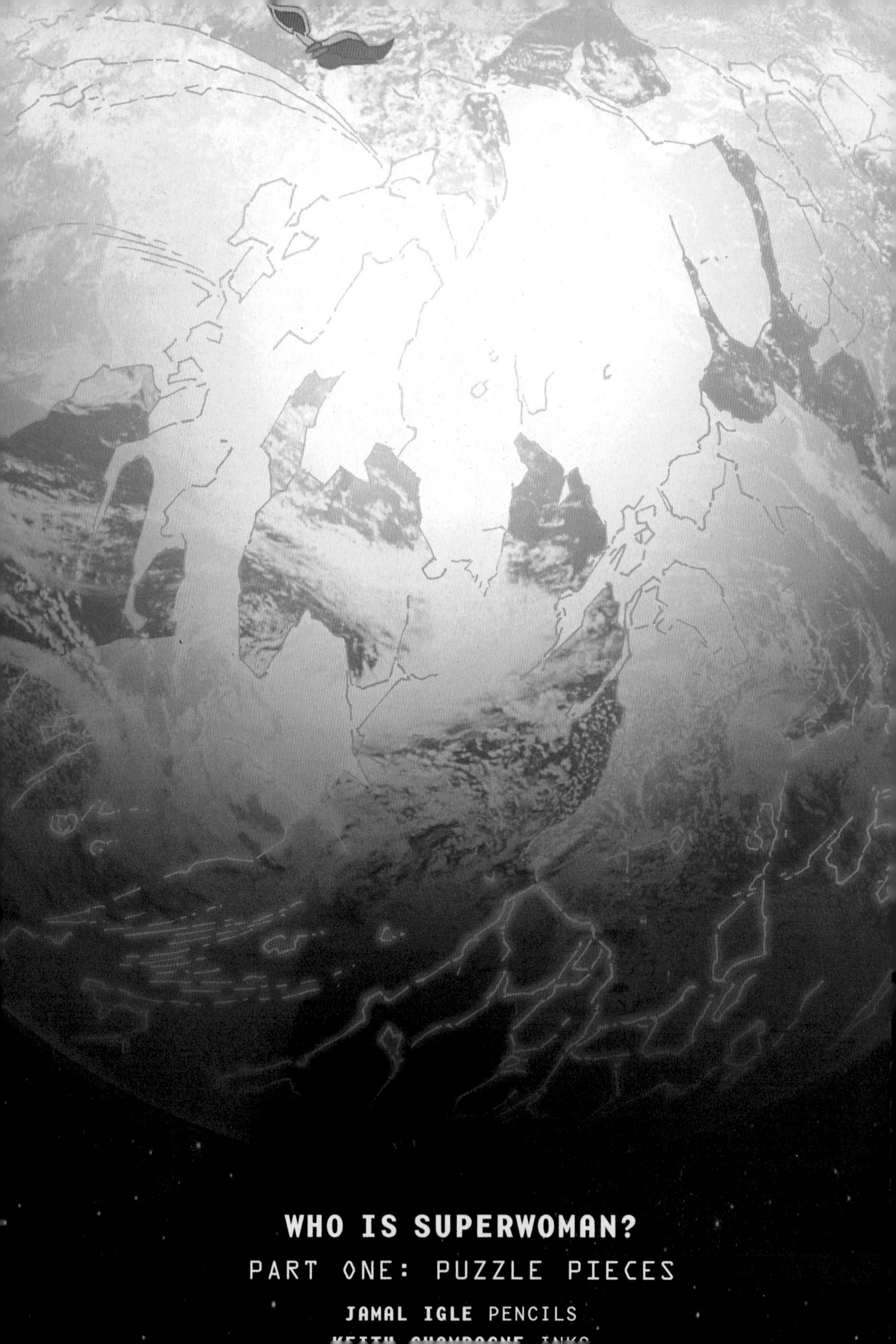

WHO IS SUPERWOMAN?

PART ONE: PUZZLE PIECES

JAMAL IGLE PENCILS

NEW KRYPTON.
THIS IS MY HOME NOW.
BECAUSE OF ARROGANCE, THE KRYPTONIAN PEOPLE HAVE LEFT THE EARTH.
THE CAPITAL CITY OF KANDOR SITS ATOP A PLANET OF ICE.
EARLY EFFORTS TO BEGIN TERRAFORMING HAVE PROVEN UNSUCCESSFUL.
THE PROUD KRYPTONIAN RACE IS BACK TO WHERE IT WAS BEFORE SUPERMAN'S INVOLVEMENT.
IN A BOTTLE ALL OVER AGAIN.

I WANT TO HELP MY PEOPLE.
MY FAMILY.
NO ONE CAN KNOW WHO I AM.
OR WHAT I'VE DONE.

A MAN ON EARTH INTIMATELY KNOWS THE KRYPTONIAN RACE.
AND HE HATES THEM.
HE UNDERSTANDS HOW TO EXPLOIT A KRYPTONIAN'S STRENGTHS--
--AS WELL AS THEIR WEAKNESSES.
...I KNOW WHO YOU ARE.

MY NAME IS
SUPERWOMAN--
--AND I'VE BEEN GIVEN ORDERS.

MY DAUGHTER IS MISSING AGAIN!
YOU'VE LET A LOT OF THINGS SLIP THROUGH YOUR SECURITY THE LAST FEW WEEKS, THARA, AND ONCE MORE, YOU'VE LOST MY DAUGHTER.
ALURA, I'M SURE WHEREVER KARA IS, SHE'S SAFE--
I DON'T CARE WHETHER YOU THINK SHE'S SAFE. I CARE THAT SHE'S NOT HERE WHEN I NEED HER TO BE.
Carrey Noble
AND COULD YOU FIND HER SOON, THARA? ALURA HAS A MISSION--
I DON'T RECALL PERSONAL SECRETARIES OUT-RANKING SECURITY CHIEFS, LYRA KAM-PAR, SO KEEP YOUR COMMENTS TO YOURSELF--
TAKE THAT TONE WITH MY NEW SECRETARY AGAIN, THARA, AND YOU MIGHT NOT BE A SECURITY CHIEF MUCH LONGER.
FIND KARA. SOON--
--BEFORE YOUR CURRENT INCOMPETENCE OUTWEIGHS THE FAITH MY HUSBAND HAD IN YOU.

I CAME OUT HERE THE FIRST TIME TO CRY.
IT'S NEXT TO IMPOSSIBLE TO FEEL LIKE YOU HAVE ANY PRIVACY IN A CITY WHERE EVERYONE HAS SUPERHEARING.
IN SPACE, THOUGH, NO ONE CAN HEAR ME GRIEVE. MY TEARS WOULD BOIL, THEN INSTANTLY FREEZE IN THE VACUUM. NO EVIDENCE OF WEEPING FOR ANYONE TO SEE.
...I MISS MY DAD.
LAST WEEK, I CAUGHT A GLIMPSE IN THE MIRROR AS I MADE MY WAY BACK TO THE CITY.
THE BOILING TEARS WERE WRECKING MY MAKEUP, SO I STOPPED MAKING THE TRIP UP.
BUT A COUPLE DAYS AGO, AFTER YET ANOTHER ARGUMENT WITH MOTHER, I DECIDED TO COME BACK...
...AND THIS TIME I NOTICED SOMETHING DIFFERENT. I LIKED BEING UP HERE. IT'S QUIET. RELAXING. ALMOST LIKE SUNBATHING.
SUNLIGHT GIVES KRYPTONIANS ENERGY, SURE, BUT IT'S ALSO COMFORTING.
LIKE RUNNING INTO AN OLD FRIEND ON THE STREET...

...OR IN THE MIDDLE OF OPEN SPACE.

EARTH.
METROPOLIS.
"EXCUSE ME, OFFICER. LOIS LANE, DAILY PLANET. MY EDITOR SENT--"
"AW, GEEZ. LANE'S HERE, GUYS!"
"SEND HER OVER TO THE NEW GUY IN CHARGE."
SIR? LOIS LANE IS--
SNF
OLD SPICE.
POLICE LINE DO NOT C
DO NOT CROS
...EXCUSE ME?
YOUR HUSBAND'S AN OLD SPICE MAN, ISN'T HE? GOOD SCENT. CLASSIC. THOUGH HE WEARS A LITTLE TOO MUCH OF IT.
WELL, I KEEP BUYING HIM OBSESSION, BUT HE SWITCHES BACK TO THE OLD STUFF WHEN I'M NOT LOOKING.
YOU'RE VERY OBSERVANT, DETECTIVE...?

INSPECTOR MIKE HENDERSON, MISS LANE. METROPOLIS METACRIMES DIVISION.
META-CRIMES...? I THOUGHT THE SCIENCE POLICE--
THE SCIPOS DO JUST WHAT THEIR NAME SAYS. THEY POLICE THE STREETS AND THE SKIES. THEY DO A FINE JOB, TOO.
I INVESTIGATE FORMS OF CRIME WHERE A METAHUMAN IS THE VICTIM.
WHY DON'T YOU TAKE A WALK WITH ME? MAYBE YOU CAN HELP US.
DIDN'T I READ AN INTERVIEW YOU WROTE WITH A SECRET SERVICE OPERATIVE NAMED BENJAMIN LOCKWOOD?
YES, AGENT LIBERTY. THE PRESIDENT'S FORMER PERSONAL BODYGUARD.
WHAT DO YOU KNOW ABOUT HIM?
NOT MUCH OUTSIDE OF HIS PRESS RELEASES.
HE WAS A CIA OPERATIVE WHO UNCOVERED A MASSIVE CONSPIRACY TO OVERTHROW OUR GOVERNMENT AND USED A SUPER-POWERED SUIT TO STOP IT.
WHEN YOU MET MR. LOCKWOOD, WHAT WAS YOUR OVERALL IMPRESSION?
HONESTLY, I DIDN'T THINK MUCH OF THE MAN. HE WAS RELUCTANT TO ANSWER ANY OF MY QUESTIONS.
AS IF HE WERE HIDING SOMETHING?
HE SEEMED... TROUBLED. DISTRACTED. I TRIED TO SCHEDULE A FOLLOW-UP INTERVIEW, BUT HE NEVER CALLED ME BACK.
WELL, MISS LANE, I'M VERY SAD TO TELL YOU THIS, BUT--

--I DON'T THINK AGENT LIBERTY'S GOING TO BE AVAILABLE FOR ANY MORE INTERVIEWS.
OH, GOD.
HIS BODY WAS FOUND TONIGHT OUT IN THE BAY.
A FISHING BOAT WAS HEADED OUT TO SEA WHEN THEIR ONBOARD COMPUTER BEGAN ACTING STRANGELY.
THEIR STEERING SEIZED UP, AND THE BOATMEN LOST ALL CONTROL OF THEIR VESSEL.
THE BOAT DROVE THEM DIRECTLY TO AGENT LIBERTY'S BODY, FLOATING FACEDOWN IN THE WATER.

MAY I SEE YOUR CELL PHONE, PLEASE?
UM, SURE.
IT SEEMS THAT IN THE EVENT OF HIS DEATH, AGENT LIBERTY'S SUIT SENDS OUT A SIGNAL THAT OVERRIDES AND CORRUPTS ELECTRONICS WITHIN A CERTAIN RADIUS.
THAT SIGNAL DREW THE BOAT IN.
I'M POSITIVE LIBERTY'S WOUNDS AREN'T SELF-INFLICTED, MISS LANE...
...BUT I THINK THE SUIT WANTS US TO KNOW THE TRUTH.
THAT AGENT LIBERTY WAS MURDERED.
SOS==--L-456-
&Ƽ--
MURDER---
MURDER---
AGENT IN
DANGER---SOS--
3456---7734---
56--AGENT
INDANGE#$$%%
--SOS--
LIBERTY IN
DAN%ER--
MURD@$#%@%
SOS--SOS--SOS

WE SPEND ANOTHER HOUR OUT IN SPACE.
HONESTLY, IT'S ONE OF THE MOST RELAXING TIMES I'VE HAD WITH ANYONE SINCE I MOVED TO NEW KRYPTON.
WE'RE JUST BEGINNING TO ENTER THE IONOSPHERE WHEN THE THOUGHT SUDDENLY HITS ME.
I HAVE NO IDEA WHO THIS WOMAN IS.
OR WHAT SHE WANTS WITH ME.
--SO WHEN I COULDN'T FIND YOU PLANETSIDE, I THOUGHT--
WHOA. YOU SEARCHED THE WHOLE PLANET FOR ME?
I'M FASTER THAN I LOOK. AND I HADN'T SEEN YOU AROUND, AND WAS STARTING TO GET CONCERNED.

CONCERNED?
AFTER... AFTER ALL THE THINGS THAT HAPPENED ON EARTH, I WAS WORRIED YOU'D TRY TO GO BACK.
TO EARTH? WHY IS THAT BAD? I HAVE A LOT OF FRIENDS ON--
THE HUMANS MADE IT CLEAR, KARA, AND THEY SPOKE LOUDLY.
THEY DON'T WANT US THERE.
INSTEAD, WE SHOULD FOCUS ON WHAT'S HAPPENING HERE. ON OUR WORLD.
NOT EVERYONE IS HAPPY THAT ALURA MADE US MOVE TO THIS PLANET.
LOOK, DO ME A FAVOR--
--DON'T GET ALL POLITIC-Y ON ME.
MY MOTHER'S CHOICES WERE MADE WITH THE GREATER GOOD OF OUR PEOPLE IN MIND.
BUT, KARA...
...DO YOU AGREE WITH HER DECISIONS?

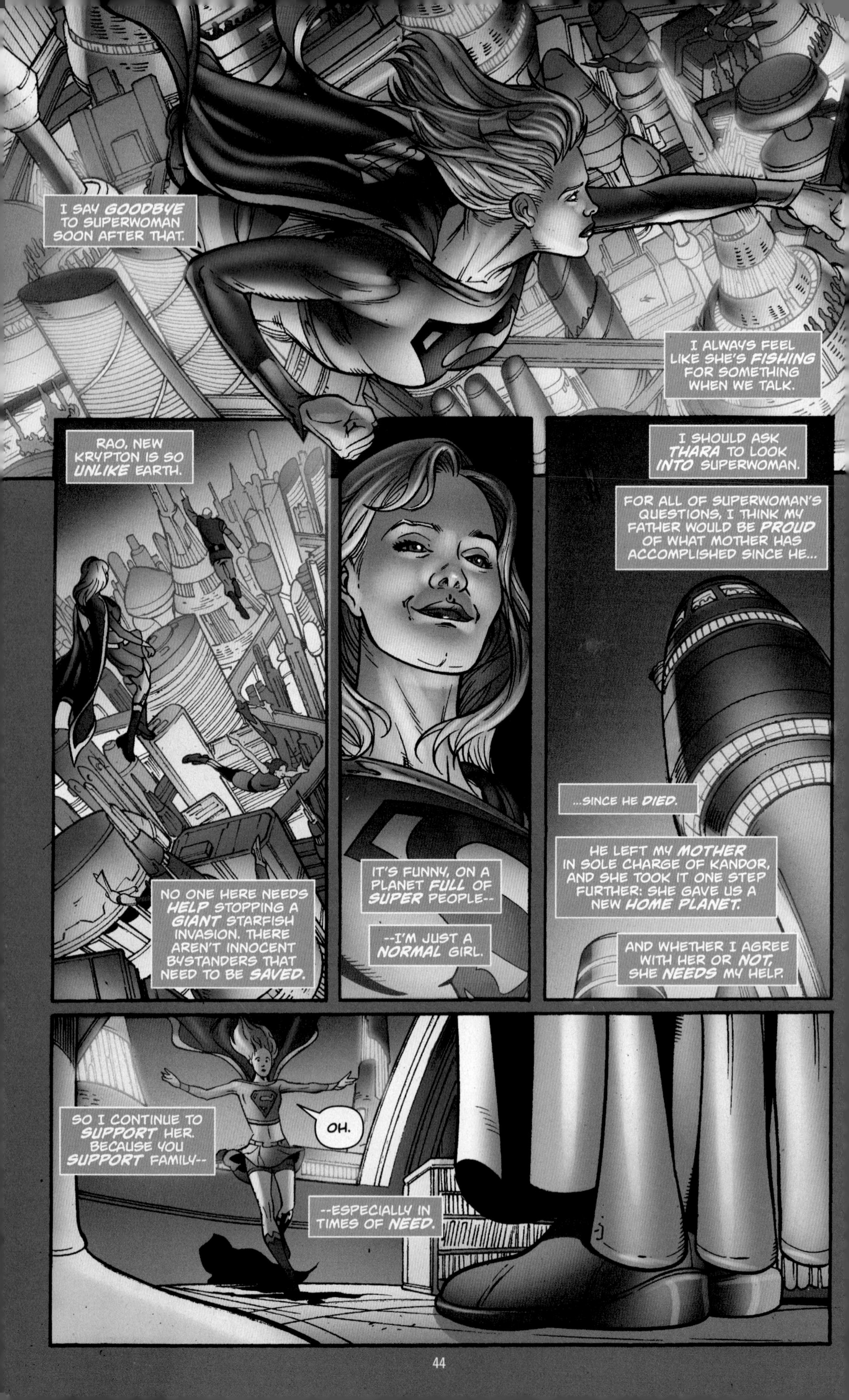
I SAY GOODBYE TO SUPERWOMAN SOON AFTER THAT.
I ALWAYS FEEL LIKE SHE'S FISHING FOR SOMETHING WHEN WE TALK.
RAO, NEW KRYPTON IS SO UNLIKE EARTH.
NO ONE HERE NEEDS HELP STOPPING A GIANT STARFISH INVASION. THERE AREN'T INNOCENT BYSTANDERS THAT NEED TO BE SAVED.
IT'S FUNNY, ON A PLANET FULL OF SUPER PEOPLE--
--I'M JUST A NORMAL GIRL.
I SHOULD ASK THARA TO LOOK INTO SUPERWOMAN.
FOR ALL OF SUPERWOMAN'S QUESTIONS, I THINK MY FATHER WOULD BE PROUD OF WHAT MOTHER HAS ACCOMPLISHED SINCE HE...
...SINCE HE DIED.
HE LEFT MY MOTHER IN SOLE CHARGE OF KANDOR, AND SHE TOOK IT ONE STEP FURTHER: SHE GAVE US A NEW HOME PLANET.
AND WHETHER I AGREE WITH HER OR NOT, SHE NEEDS MY HELP.
SO I CONTINUE TO SUPPORT HER. BECAUSE YOU SUPPORT FAMILY--
OH.
--ESPECIALLY IN TIMES OF NEED.

UM, HI.
I WAS JUST, AH, OUT--
Meteors
FOLLOW ME.
NOW.
I DON'T WANT TO KNOW WHERE YOU'VE BEEN, BUT I DO NEED TO KNOW I CAN TRUST YOU, KARA.
I'M SORRY, I JUST WENT OUT. I DIDN'T THINK IT WOULD BE A BIG DEAL--
WE'LL DISCUSS PUNISHMENT LATER.
PUNISHMENT?
RIGHT NOW, I HAVE A JOB FOR YOU.
A JOB?
I'M SENDING YOU TO EARTH.

TO EARTH? WHY?
THE HUMAN KNOWN AS REACTRON REMAINS FREE.
I WANT YOU TO BRING HIM TO ME.
YOU DON'T HAVE TO DO THIS, KARA--
I DISAGREE.
SHE VERY MUCH HAS TO DO THIS.
WHY--WHY DO YOU WANT HIM? WHAT DO YOU WANT HIM FOR?
YOU WERE SPYING ON THE MILITARY?
MONITORING THEM.
AFTER REVIEWING OUR INTEL, WE DISCOVERED A MESSAGE SENT FROM A MAJOR BENJAMIN KRULL TO A WOMAN IN METROPOLIS NAMED LORI MURPHY.
HE CLAIMED HE WAS GOING TO BE IN METROPOLIS TODAY, EARTH-TIME, AND THAT HE WANTED TO SEE HER.
AFTER FURTHER REVIEW OF OUR INTEL, WE FOUND THAT MAJOR KRULL USED TO GO BY THE CODE NAME "REACTRON."
KRULL IS THE MAN WHO KILLED ZOR-EL.

HE ASSASSINATED YOUR FATHER, KARA. HE MURDERED THE LEADER OF KANDOR IN ITS STREETS.
WE CAN'T ALLOW HIM TO ROAM FREELY.
BUT WE DON'T EVEN KNOW WHERE HE IS.
HE DISAPPEARED SECONDS AFTER-- AFTER THE ATTACK, AND NEITHER KAL NOR I COULD FIND HIM--
HMPH. THARA?
ON YOUR MOTHER'S ORDERS, MY TEAM WAS MONITORING CERTAIN HUMAN MILITARY CHANNELS BEFORE WE LEFT EARTH.
UR MISSION, KARA, IS OF E UTMOST IMPORTANCE AND DEMANDS THE HIGHEST LEVEL OF SECRECY.
YOU WILL GO METROPOLIS AND FETCH REACTRON.
TELL NO ONE YOU'RE GOING. NO KRYPTONIAN OUTSIDE THIS ROOM WILL KNOW OF YOUR MISSION.
CAN I TRUST YOU WITH THIS TASK?
I-I--
I'LL GO.

"DON'T GO, KARA. WHAT DO YOU THINK ALURA'S GOING TO DO TO HIM ONCE SHE GETS HIM?"
YOU HEARD HER. IMPRISON HIM FOR HIS CRIME.
YOU'RE BEING NAIVE. YOUR MOTHER'S NOT GOING TO STOP AT IMPRISONING HIM.
SHE HAS NO RESPECT FOR HUMAN LIFE. HE'LL BE EXECUTED--
HE KILLED MY FATHER, THARA. I HAVE TO GO.
AND IF YOU HAVE PROBLEMS WITH WORKING FOR MY MOTHER, THEN MAYBE YOU SHOULDN'T ANYMORE...
YOU'RE RIGHT. MAYBE I SHOULDN'T.
GOODBYE, KARA--
"--I WON'T WISH YOU LUCK."

"DON'T WORRY ABOUT IT, SMALLVILLE."
I'LL COVER. PERRY WON'T EVEN NOTICE YOU'RE GONE.
GOOD LUCK AT STRYKER'S TODAY.
NO, I CAN'T. I'VE GOT A CALL. I LOVE YOU, TOO.
HI, THIS IS LOIS LANE FROM THE DAILY PLANET. I'M LOOKING FOR INSPECTOR MIKE HENDERSON?
YES, I CAN HOLD.
INSPECTOR? LOIS LANE, DAILY PLANET.
I WAS HOPING TO GET A FEW QUOTES FROM YOU ABOUT AGENT LIBERTY--
I'M SORRY, BUT I CAN'T TALK, MISS LANE.
"WE'RE ABOUT TO START AGENT LIBERTY'S AUTOPSY."

UNNH--!
KRAK
SUPERWOMAN?! WHAT THE ⊣⊢·T⌂◊ ARE YOU DOING?
I CAN'T LET YOU GO ANY FARTHER, KARA.
YOU CAN'T BE ON EARTH!
WHAT? WHY NOT?
"IT'S TOO DANGEROUS FOR YOU TO BE HERE!"
HELLO?
LORI? IT'S BENJAMIN.
I BEEN DYING TO SEE YOU, BABY.

I'LL LEAVE WHEN I'M READY TO, SUPERWOMAN.
KARA, PLEASE.
QUIT.
NOW, GET OUT OF MY WAY AND GO BACK TO NEW KRYPTON.
I'M GOING TO METROPOLIS--
REMEMBER THAT I TRIED.
WHAT?

THOOM

WHO IS SUPERWOMAN?

PART TWO: CLASHES

JAMAL IGLE PENCILS
KEITH CHAMPAGNE INKS

ORIGINS & OMENS

MATTHEW CLARK ARTIST

EARTH.
MILES OVER THE EASTERN SEABOARD.
MY MOTHER SENT ME ON A MISSION TO EARTH TO FIND MY FATHER'S KILLER.
THE MAN WITH THE KRYPTONITE TOUCH. REACTRON.
I'M SUPPOSED TO BE IN METROPOLIS RIGHT NOW, TRACKING HIM DOWN.
DON'T FIGHT ME ON THIS, KARA!
INSTEAD, A WOMAN I BARELY KNOW IS DOING HER BEST TO STOP ME AND SEND ME HOME.
I TOLD YOU--

I'M SUPERGIRL
--YOU'VE GOT TO GO BACK TO NEW KRYPTON!

THIS IS MY LIFE.

ALL RIGHT, STOP! STOP!
I'LL GO WITH YOU!
THANK RAO. IF WE HURRY, WE CAN BE BACK ON NEW KRYPTON BEFORE ANYBODY--
PSYCHE!

LEAVE ME ALONE!
BOOOOM
IF I HURRY, I CAN BE IN METROPOLIS IN SEC--
SHIIINNG
...

IT'LL BE OKAY.
YOU'VE JUST GOT TO TRUST ME.
KSSSHH
IT'S IMPORTANT YOU LEAVE EARTH AS SOON AS POSSIBLE.
YOU DON'T KNOW WHAT COULD HAPPEN WHILE YOU'RE OFF NEW KRYPT--
FZZZT
I'M SO GOING TO KICK YOU IN THE FACE!

DO YOU EVER LISTEN TO OTHER PEOPLE, KARA?!
I TOLD YOU NOT TO COME BACK HERE!
NO MATTER WHAT YOUR MOTHER SAID!
WHAT? THARA? IS THAT--
SPLSHH

KRSHHHHH
VEE VEE VEE VEE
ᗒKZZTᗕ THIS LINE ᗒKZZTᗕ SECURE?
IT BROADCASTS ON A FREQUENCY ONLY I CAN HEAR.
ᗒKZZZAATTᗕ WE'VE DETECTED YOU ON EARTH ᗒZZTTᗕ
I CAME TO RETREIVE KARA ZOR-EL, AND I'M RETURNING HER TO NEW KRYPTON--
ᗒKZZTTᗕ LEAVE HER WHERE YOU ARE ᗒKZZTᗕ
WHAT? WHY? I CAN HAVE HER OFFWORLD IN MINUTES--
DROP HER RIGHT NOWWWZZZTᗕ THAT'S AN ORDER. YOU'RE NEEDED ELSE-WHERE--
ᗒKZZZVTTᗕ THERE'S A STRAY DOG I NEED YOU TO CATCH ᗒZZZTᗕ
UNDERSTOOD.

GO HOME, KARA.
"CUT SLOWLY--"

METROPOLIS CITY HOSPITAL.
SURGICAL UNIT.
--YOU DON'T WANT TO DAMAGE THE BODY INSIDE.
I UNDERSTAND WHY WE'RE CUTTING AGENT LIBERTY OUT OF HIS SUIT, INSPECTOR HENDERSON, BUT WHY ALL OF THESE ELECTRODES?
VREEEEEEEEEEEEEEE
AGENT LIBERTY'S UNIFORM IS AN ADVANCED BIOMETRIC POWER SUIT. WHILE SOME-ONE IS IN IT, IT RESPONDS ONLY TO THEIR COMMANDS.
THE TECH BOYS THINK IF WE CAN CUT HIM OUT OF IT--
--THE INTERNAL COMPUTER WILL UNLOCK AND WE'LL BE ABLE TO ACCESS ITS MEMORY.
LEXCOMP
LEXCOMP
THIS GUY WAS A PRETTY BIG HERO BACK IN THE DAY, HUH?
MM. HUGE. HE SAVED A LOT OF PEOPLE'S LIVES.
FOR THEIR SAKE, I'M GOING TO SOLVE THIS MURDER--
WHAT IS THIS?

EVERYONE, STOP WHAT YOU'RE DOING!
WE'RE HERE FOR AGENT LIBERTY'S BODY.
WAIT A MINUTE, WHO DO YOU THINK YOU ARE--?
I'M MAJOR LUCY LANE.
I'VE BEEN ASSIGNED BY THE PRESIDENT OF THE UNITED STATES TO INVESTIGATE AGENT LIBERTY'S DISAPPEARANCE, AND I FIND HIM IN A METROPOLIS MORGUE BEING FLAYED BY SOME COP.
YOU CAN'T JUST MARCH IN HERE AND--
CAN AND WILL, INSPECTOR.
AGENT LIBERTY WAS THE PRESIDENT'S BODYGUARD AND A MEMBER OF THE SECRET SERVICE. ONE OF OURS.
THE MOMENT YOU FOUND HIS BODY, YOU SHOULD'VE REPORTED IT. WHAT WERE YOU THINKING?
BE THANKFUL HE COMMISSIONER VOUCHED SO ASSIONATELY FOR OU AND YOUR WORK, THERWISE I WOULD HAVE YOU ARRESTED.
THIS APERWORK ETAILS OUR RIGHT TO LIBERTY'S BODY.
MY INVESTIGATION INTO HIS MURDER WILL BE ONGOING.
I TRUST THAT IF YOU OBTAIN ANY MORE INFORMATION REGARDING HIS CASE, YOU'LL CONTACT ME.
MY NUMBER IS IN THE FILE.
MAJOR LANE. ANY RELATION TO LOIS LANE?
LANE

SHE'S MY SISTER. WHY?
MET HER THE OTHER DAY. NICE GIRL.
GOOD TO KNOW YOUR DADDY RAISED AT LEAST ONE OF YOU TO HAVE SOME MANNERS.
...
GOOD DAY, INSPECTOR.
MEMORY DOWN
COMPLETED

HOLD THE FRONT PAGE, PERRY!
THE U.N. JUST BANNED ALL KRYPTONIANS FROM EARTH EXCEPT SUPERMAN!
I'M TYPING UP THE STORY RIGHT NOW--
OH, MY.
WHO SENT THIS?

OH, THE MAILROOM GUYS BROUGHT THAT UP WHILE YOU WERE AWAY, MS. GRANT.
FROM "MY TINIEST FAN"? WHO COULD THAT--
WOW. ISN'T THAT... SOMETHING?
WELL, IT'S A NICE GESTURE--
--BUT I'M A LITTLE TOO MATURE TO PLAY WITH DOLLS.
CAT! WHAT'S THE E.T.A. ON THAT ARTICLE!?
COMING, PERRY!

WHAT ARE THEY THINKING, MARTHA?
RYPTONIANS BANNED BY UNITED NAT
ONCE THIS GOES INTO EFFECT, KARA WON'T BE ABLE TO COME BACK--
MARTHA, HOLD ON A SECOND.
NOCK NOCK NOCK
KARA!
...HEY, LANA...I FR'GOT...
...MY KEYS...
"STAY AWAY FROM ME, BEN!"

I WANT YOU BACK OUT OF MY LIFE!
OH, LORI, LORI, LORI. YOU ARE MELODRAMA INCARNATE.
JUST LIKE BEFORE.
BEFORE I GOT SICK. BEFORE YOU LEFT ME.
KLKSSSSS
NO, I WOULDN'T BE TOO CONCERNED ABOUT HAVING ME BACK IN YOUR LIFE FOR MUCH LONGER, HONEYBABY.
IN FACT, IF I WERE YOU--
--I'D BE MORE CONCERNED WITH HOW LITTLE LIFE YOU HAVE LEFT.
VMMMMMMM

KRAKOOOOM!
REACTRON!
I'VE BEEN SENT TO RETRIEVE YOU.
OH, GREAT. THE TURNCOAT KRYPTONIAN. HE SENT YOU TO PICK ME UP AGAIN?
LOOK, I APPRECIATED THE LIFT OUT OF KANDOR, BUT TELL GENERAL LANE TO COOL HIS HEELS.
I'VE TAKEN A TEMPORARY LEAVE OF--
HURK
IT'S TIME FOR US TO GO.
WRRR
OH, NO, KRYPTONIAN.
ME AND MY LITTLE GOLD KRYPTONITE FRIEND HERE--

--WE SAY IT'S TIME FOR YOU TO FRY.
SHRAKK
HN. TICKLED.
HRKKK
H-HOW? GOLD KRYPTONITE SHUH--
--SHUTS OFF KRYPTONIAN POWERS.
WHY, REACTRON--
--WHOEVER SAID I WAS KRYPTONIAN?

I AM SCAR.
I AM ONE OF THE GUARDIANS OF THE UNIVERSE, THOUGH THAT TITLE GROWS MORE MEANINGLESS TO ME EVERY DAY.
ONCE HE IS HERE, I WILL HAVE A NEW CALLING.
WHILE I WAIT, I WRITE IN THE BOOK OF THE BLACK.
I WRITE OF THOSE IMPORTANT ENOUGH TO GRACE ITS PAGES.
I WRITE OF THEIR FEARS.
AND THEIR DESIRES.
AND THEIR INEVITABLE DOWNFALLS.
SHE WAS ONCE A LOYAL MEMBER OF THE GUARDIANS OF THE UNIVERSE, FOUNDERS OF THE GREEN LANTERN CORPS. BUT SINCE SHE BURNED AT THE HAND OF THE ANTI-MONITOR, HER SOUL ROTS WITH DARKNESS. UNBEKNOWNST TO HER FELLOW OANS, HER LOYALTIES NOW LIE ELSEWHERE. THE GUARDIANS OF THE UNIVERSE TAKE NO NAMES, YET SOON THIS ONE WILL BE KNOWN AS
SCAR
KARA ZOR-EL.
TEENAGED SUPERGIRL OF EARTH.
DAUGHTER OF NEW KRYPTON.
TORN BETWEEN TWO PLANETS.
WILL SHE ALONE BE ABLE TO UNITE THOSE DISPARATE WORLDS?
OR WILL THE BURDEN OF CHOICE OVERWHELM HER?
ORIGINS & OMENS

I JUST DON'T KNOW.
IN ONE DIRECTION IS A PLANET FULL OF ANGRY HUMANS, MOST OF WHOM DON'T LIKE KRYPTONIANS RIGHT NOW. OR ME.
IF ANYONE ON EARTH EVEN SEES MY "S," THEY'LL PROBABLY SHOOT TO KILL.
IN THE OTHER DIRECTION IS A PLANET FULL OF MY ANGRY MOTHER.
...I'D ALMOST RATHER DEAL WITH THE HUMANS.
FLOATING OUT HERE HOLDING MY BREATH ISN'T GOING TO SOLVE ANYTHING, THOUGH.
I REALLY JUST NEED TO--
CHOOSE.
WHAT? LANA?
CHOOSE.
YES. CHOOSE.

MOM?!
CHOOSE.
CHOOSE.
LET GO!
CHOOSE!
CHOOSE!
CHOOSE!
CHOOSE!
STOP!
STOP!
"SO WHAT'S IT LIKE OVER THERE?"

ON NEW KRYPTON? IT'S... DIFFERENT.
OUR PEOPLE ARE HAPPY THERE. THE PLANET ITSELF IS BEAUTIFUL, TOO, BUT...
IT'S WEIRD, BUT BEING AROUND OTHER KRYPTONIANS LIKE MY MOTHER, I'M REALLY STARTING TO FEEL...WELL...
ALIEN?
SOME OF THEM ARE SO DIFFERENT FROM HUMANS, LANA. THEY THINK DIFFERENTLY, THEY SPEAK DIFFERENTLY, THEY... REACT DIFFERENTLY.
I'VE BEEN ON EARTH SO LONG, IT'S BEEN HARD FOR ME TO FALL BACK INTO BEING "JUST ANOTHER KRYPTONIAN."
BUT MOTHER NEEDS ME THERE, WITH DAD... GONE...
WELL, IF YOU WANT TO STAY HERE, KARA, YOU CAN. INDEFINITELY.
I KNOW YOUR MOTHER DOESN'T APPROVE OF YOUR EARTH IDENTITY, BUT THIS IS LINDA LANG'S APARTMENT, TOO.
BESIDES, IT'LL BE NICE TO HAVE SOMEONE ELSE AROUND TO CHANGE STREAKY'S LITTER BO--
KAFF KAFF KAFF
LANA?

NNN.
...IT'S... I'M FINE. THE... COFFEE CREAMER MUST'VE GONE BAD.
LIKE I WAS SAYING, YOU'RE ALWAYS WELCOME HERE, KARA.
I KNOW IT'S BEEN HARD FOR YOU SINCE ZOR-EL WAS KILLED, AND YOU'RE FOCUSING ALL YOUR EFFORTS ON PULLING YOUR MOTHER OUT OF HER SLUMP...
BUT, KARA, IT'S OKAY TO BE SELFISH SOMETIMES. IF YOU WANT TO STAY HERE ON EARTH, YOU CAN.
DO WHAT YOU NEED TO DO TO DEAL.
I LEARNED A LONG TIME AGO, SOMETIMES THE BEST THING YOU CAN GIVE THE GRIEVING--
"--IS SPACE."
HER FRIENDS OFFER HER THEIR COMPASSION--

--BUT THEY WILL NOT ALWAYS BE THERE TO SUPPORT HER.
ONCE THEY ARE GONE, FROM WHOM WILL KARA ZOR-EL DRAW HOPE?
EVEN NOW, HER ENEMIES ARE MOBILIZING, AND HER GREATEST FEARS HAVE BEGUN TO SEE THE LIGHT.
SOON, SHE WILL BE CRIPPLED BY INDECISION, AND BOTH THE KRYPTONIANS AND THE HUMANS WILL SEE HER FOR WHAT SHE TRULY IS--

--A SCARED LITTLE GIRL.
SO IT IS WRITTEN.

SO IT SHALL BE.

WHO IS SUPERWOMAN?

PART THREE: TICKING CLOCKS

JAMAL IGLE TALENT CALDWELL PENCILS
JON SIBAL TALENT CALDWELL INKS

METROPOLIS.
3815 MOONEY DRIVE. APARTMENT 6B.
WHAT I AM UNDER THIS MASK, REACTRON, ISN'T YOUR CONCERN. GATHER YOUR THINGS.
HHH
SO Y-YOU'RE NOT KRYPTONIAN UNDER THERE?
WE NEED TO GO BEFORE THE SCIENCE POLICE OR THEIR CAMERAS ARRIVE.
I CAN'T BE SEEN HERE.
NNNN
OH, GOOD MORNING, SUNSHINE.
ALMOST FORGOT TO SAY GOODBYE BEFORE WE LEFT.
KKKRRKKKLL

SHRAKK

STAND DOWN!

IDIOT!
KRAK
I WAS GIVEN TWO SPECIFIC ORDERS FOR THIS MISSION, KRULL.
"ONE: RETRIEVE THE AWOL CODENAME: REACTRON FROM GIRLFRIEND'S HOME IN METROPOLIS."
"GIRLFRIEND"?! I BARELY KNOW HIM!
KK
NOW LET GO OF ME, SUPERFREAK!
DO YOU WANT ME TO GIVE YOU BACK TO HIM?
N-NO.
THEN DON'T TEST ME, GIRL.
HRR.
W-WHAT WAS LANE'S OTHER ORDER?

"TWO:"
SHRRRKKK
KRNNK
HHHHHHHH
W-WHAT?
"MAKE SURE HER DEATH LOOKS ACCIDENTAL."
WAIT!
I THOUGHT-- CGHCGH CGH
I THOUGHT YOU WERE HERE TO SAVE ME!
VZZT
WHY AREN'T YOU SAVING M--

WHY CAN'T YOU ASK YOUR FRIENDS FOR HELP? THE TEEN TITANS?
I TOLD YOU, I'M ON A MISSION NO ONE CAN HELP ME WITH. NOT CASSIE, NOT ROBIN.
NOT EVEN KAL.
MY MOTHER TOLD ME NOT TO TELL ANYONE WHY I CAME BACK.
SOMEONE MUST'VE TOLD SOMEONE WHO TOLD SOMEONE ELSE, THOUGH, BECAUSE SUPERWOMAN WAS WAITING FOR ME HERE ON EARTH.
SHE KNOCKED ME OUT AND DUMPED ME IN THE ATLANTIC, EXACTLY THE THING A FRIEND WOULDN'T DO.
SHE KEPT ME FROM MY MISSION, BUT I'M BACK ON THE TRAIL OF REACTRON.
I NEEDED HELP, SO I TURNED TO THE ONLY HUMAN I KNOW I CAN ABSOLUTELY TRUST--
DAILY PLANET
KRYPTONIANS, GO HOME!
An article by Cat Grant
"NEWS THAT MAKES THE WORLD GO ROUND EVERY DAY IN THE DAILY PLANET"
MAURICE BROS
AVENUE A

--LANA LANG.
I HAVE TO FIND THIS WOMAN, AND I HAVE TO FIND HER QUICKLY. IT'S IMPORTANT.
OKAY, HONEY. I BELIEVE YOU. BUT YOU CAN'T BE SEEN IN METROPOLIS. KRYPTONIANS HAVE BEEN BANNED--
I KNOW, I SAW CAT'S ARTICLE. I'M REALLY STARTING TO DISLIKE THAT WOMAN. DON'T WORRY--
--I'M FLYING FAST ENOUGH NO ONE CAN SEE ME. HOW MANY MORE ON THE LIST?
I'VE BEEN TO SIX DIFFERENT APARTMENTS TODAY AND MET SIX DIFFERENT WOMEN SHARING THE NAME "LORI MURPHY."
DAILY PLANET
KRYPTONIANS, GO HOME!
A QUICK CLOTHES CHANGE AND A FEW QUESTIONS ASKED YIELDED NOTHING. NONE OF THEM KNEW BENJAMIN KRULL.
THERE ARE TWO MORE LORI MURPHYS LISTED IN METROPOLIS.
ONE LIVES IN AN APARTMENT COMPLEX AT THE CORNER OF BINDER AND MOONEY, AND THE OTHER ONE'S FARTHER UPTOWN.
GREAT--
BUT I KNOW HIM. AND IF I FIND THE RIGHT LORI MURPHY, I'LL FIND REACTRON.
--I'LL HEAD DOWNTOWN FIRST.

MS. LANG, I REALLY SHOULD GET BACK TO MY RESEARCH--
NONSENSE, HARRISON. YOU WORK FOR ME, AND MY NIECE NEEDS HELP TODAY.
HER NAME'S LINDA, RIGHT? HOT IN A "SEXY LIBRARIAN" KINDA WAY?
ONE MORE WORD ABOUT MY NIECE, HARRISON, AND YOU'RE VERY, VERY FIRED.
WHAT'S THE NEXT ADDRESS ON THE LIST?
KAR--LINDA? EVERYTHING OKAY?
THIS IS THE RIGHT APARTMENT--

--BUT I'M TOO LATE.
THERE WAS A FIRE. I THINK SHE'S...
A FIRE? IF THERE ARE FIRE-FIGHTERS OR POLICE AROUND, YOU SHOULD GET OUT OF THERE.
YEAH, BUT...
...I NEED TO SEE...
LANA, I THINK SHE'S DEAD.
THERE'S NO WAY THIS WAS AN ACCIDENT.
YOU NEED TO LEAVE BEFORE ANYONE CATCHES SIGHT OF YOU.
I'M GOOD AS GONE. BUT DON'T FREAK--
7734-5
"--NO ONE SAW ME."

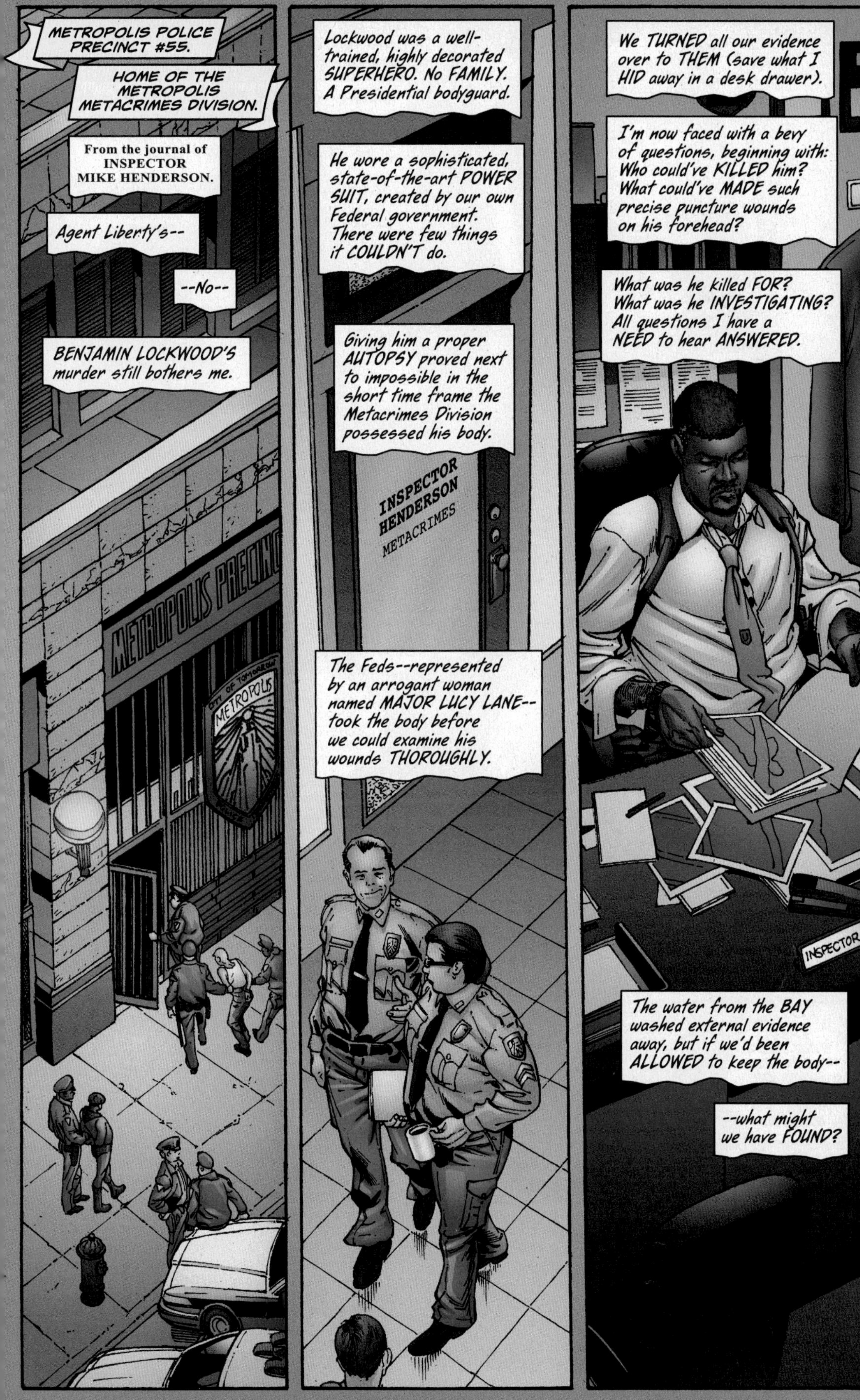
METROPOLIS POLICE PRECINCT #55.
HOME OF THE METROPOLIS METACRIMES DIVISION.
From the journal of INSPECTOR MIKE HENDERSON.
Agent Liberty's--
--No--
BENJAMIN LOCKWOOD'S murder still bothers me.
METROPOLIS PRECINC
METROPOLIS
Lockwood was a well-trained, highly decorated SUPERHERO. No FAMILY. A Presidential bodyguard.
He wore a sophisticated, state-of-the-art POWER SUIT, created by our own Federal government. There were few things it COULDN'T do.
Giving him a proper AUTOPSY proved next to impossible in the short time frame the Metacrimes Division possessed his body.
INSPECTOR HENDERSON
METACRIMES
The Feds--represented by an arrogant woman named MAJOR LUCY LANE--took the body before we could examine his wounds THOROUGHLY.
We TURNED all our evidence over to THEM (save what I HID away in a desk drawer).
I'm now faced with a bevy of questions, beginning with: Who could've KILLED him? What could've MADE such precise puncture wounds on his forehead?
What was he killed FOR? What was he INVESTIGATING? All questions I have a NEED to hear ANSWERED.
INSPECTOR
The water from the BAY washed external evidence away, but if we'd been ALLOWED to keep the body--
--what might we have FOUND?

Maybe I'll NEVER know. Like MEN have LOVERS that get away, cops have cases they look back on with WISTFUL eyes.
Whenever CAPTAIN TANNER would get a few drinks in him, he'd talk about the one case he NEVER solved, where a small boy was KILLED by the sound of a WOMAN'S VOICE--
AGENT LIBERTY
SIR?
THE TECH GUYS JUST CALLED UP ASKING FOR YOU.
TELL THEM I'M BUSY.
I DID, SIR, BUT THEY INSISTED YOU COME DOWN. SAID THE WEIRDEST THING, TOO.
OH?
THEY SAID THEY RECOVERED SOME OF AGENT LIBERTY'S MEMORY.
DOES THAT MEAN ANYTHING TO YOU, SIR?
...SIR?

HAMMERSMITH TOWER.
APARTMENT OF LANA AND LINDA LANG.
MOTHER.

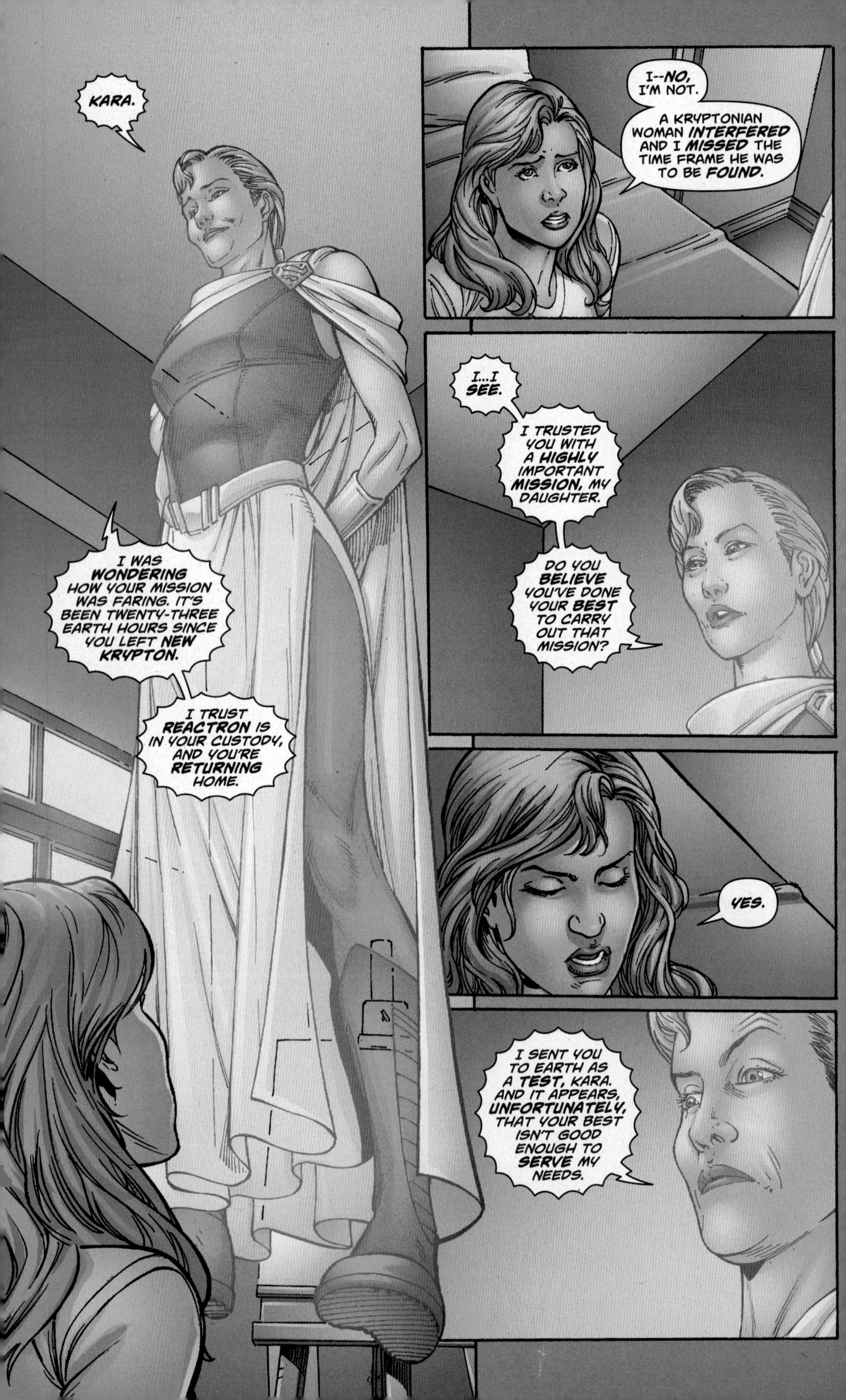
KARA.
I WAS WONDERING HOW YOUR MISSION WAS FARING. IT'S BEEN TWENTY-THREE EARTH HOURS SINCE YOU LEFT NEW KRYPTON.
I TRUST REACTRON IS IN YOUR CUSTODY, AND YOU'RE RETURNING HOME.
I--NO, I'M NOT.
A KRYPTONIAN WOMAN INTERFERED AND I MISSED THE TIME FRAME HE WAS TO BE FOUND.
I...I SEE.
I TRUSTED YOU WITH A HIGHLY IMPORTANT MISSION, MY DAUGHTER.
DO YOU BELIEVE YOU'VE DONE YOUR BEST TO CARRY OUT THAT MISSION?
YES.
I SENT YOU TO EARTH AS A TEST, KARA. AND IT APPEARS, UNFORTUNATELY, THAT YOUR BEST ISN'T GOOD ENOUGH TO SERVE MY NEEDS.

KARA?
...CAN'T SAY THINGS LIKE THAT TO ME, MOTHER!
I TOLD YOU, THIS ISN'T MY FAULT! THERE WAS A KRYPTONIAN WOMAN--
ENOUGH.
ONE MORE CHANCE. BRING ME REACTRON. YOU OWE IT TO YOUR FATHER'S MEMORY.
IF THERE'S ANOTHER KRYPTONIAN ON EARTH, BRING THEM TO ME, TOO.
THEY MUSTN'T BE ALLOWED TO TRAIPSE BACK AND FORTH BETWEEN WORLDS THE WAY YOUR COUSIN HAS BEEN.
I WARN YOU. DO NOT RETURN TO NEW KRYPTON EMPTY-HANDED, KARA.
DO NOT LET ANYONE OR ANYTHING KEEP YOU FROM YOUR TASK.
IF YOU PASS THIS TEST, YOU WILL PROVE TO ME THAT YOU ARE NOT AS USELESS A SOLDIER AS SOME WOULD LEAD ME TO BELIEVE--
MOTHER.
SHUT UP!
KKRAKKSH

HEY.
HOW MUCH OF THAT DID YOU HEAR?
MOST OF IT.
LANA, WHAT'S WRONG WITH HER? WHY IS SHE SO HORRIBLE TO ME?
I DO WHAT SHE ASKS. I TRY SO HARD TO HELP HER, AND ALL I GET IS HER ANGER. HER DISAPPROVAL. SHE WASN'T LIKE THIS WHEN DAD WAS ALIVE.
I CAN'T HELP BUT WONDER, LANA...
WHY CUH--
...WHY COULDN'T HE HAVE KILLED HER INSTEAD OF FATHER?

PROJECT 7734.
I TRUST YOU HAD NO TROUBLE WITH REACTRON?
NONE. THE SUIT HELD AGAINST HIS KRYPTONITE BLASTS. AS I THOUGHT IT WOULD.
AND IF IT HADN'T HELD?
LET'S HOPE WE NEVER LEARN.
IS GENERAL LANE HERE, LIEUTENANT HOLLISTER?
NO, SUPERWOMAN. THE GENERAL IS PREOCCUPIED WITH ANOTHER MATTER AND REGRETS NOT BEING HERE TO MEET YOU PERSONALLY.
HE DID, HOWEVER, ASK ME TO ISSUE YOU YOUR NEXT ASSIGNMENT.
I'M WORKING WITH HIM NOW?
THAT'S WHAT THEY TOLD ME, TOO, SUPER-BUMPS.
CLASSIFIED
YOU AND ME'RE GOING ON A DATE--
CLASSIFIED
--AND WE'RE GONNA MAKE IT A THREESOME BEFORE IT'S ALL SAID AND DONE.

--I HEAR IN GOTHAM, THEY GOT A SIGNAL FOR THIS KINDA THING.
YOU SURE HE'LL BE HERE?
LOIS LANE PROMISED ME SHE'D SEND SOMEONE ALONG WHO CAN HELP.
WELL, WHAT'S THAT S'POSED TO MEAN?
SHE WAS UNCLEAR ON THE PHONE, BUT I HAVE NO REASON NOT TO BELIEVE HER.
UM, I REALLY HATE DISAPPOINTING PEOPLE--
--BUT MY COUSIN'S OFF-PLANET, SO SHE CALLED ME INSTEAD. SORRY.
GEEZ! KRYPTONIAN!
THIS IS PROBABLY A BAD IDEA.

YOU GOT THE RIGHT TO REMAIN SILENT--
STOP, BROYLES.
YEAH. DEFINITELY A BAD ONE.
BUT, SIR, SHE'S AN ILLEGAL ALIEN--
I KNOW.
BUT SIR, WHAT ABOUT THOSE SCIENCE POLICEMEN--!
SUPERGIRL DIDN'T KILL THOSE MEN, BROYLES.
YOU SAID SUPERMAN'S OFF THE PLANET?
YES.
THEN YOU'LL HAVE TO DO. BROYLES?
SIR?
WE CAN'T WALK HER THROUGH THE BUILDING DRESSED LIKE THAT.
"I'M NOT SURE WHY I'M HERE, INSPECTOR."

I'VE NEVER EVEN MET AGENT LIBERTY--
I WON'T LIE. I HAD HOPED FOR YOUR COUSIN, BUT I THINK YOU CAN ANSWER SOME OF MY QUESTIONS.
LIBERTY'S COSTUME WAS AN EXTREMELY ADVANCED POWER SUIT, EQUIPPED WITH ALL MANNER OF SURVEILLANCE AND RECORDING DEVICES.
AGENT LIBERTY'S AUDIO AND VISUAL FEEDS WERE CONSTANTLY RECORDED AND BURNED ONTO HIS SUIT'S HARD DRIVE.
UNFORTUNATELY, BETWEEN HIS INJURIES AND THE WATER FROM THE BAY, THAT DATA WAS CORRUPTED. HOWEVER--
--AFTER CONSIDERABLE EFFORTS MADE BY MY TEAM, WE WERE ABLE TO PULL OFF THE LAST IMAGE HE RECORDED.
THE SUIT--
RECORDED HIS MURDERER. WE HAVE A PHOTOGRAPH OF HER.
WHICH IS WHY I NEED TO KNOW MORE ABOUT YOUR FAMILY.
WHAT?
PUBLIC RECORD SAYS THAT SYMBOL YOU AND SUPERMAN WEAR ON YOUR CHESTS IS A FAMILY CREST. SO, TELL ME--
--WHO IS SUPERWOMAN? AND WHY WOULD SOMEONE FROM YOUR FAMILY KILL AGENT LIBERTY?
YES, SUPER-GIRL--

--WHY WOULD YOUR FAMILY WANT AGENT LIBERTY DEAD? WHAT DID HE DISCOVER ABOUT YOUR FAMILY'S TRUE INTENTIONS ON EARTH?
MAJOR LANE?
INSPECTOR. DIDN'T THINK I'D SEE YOU SO SOON--
LANE
CONFERENCE ROOM 105
--BUT ONE OF YOUR MEN SAW FIT TO REPORT IN TO US THAT YOU WERE HARBORING AN ILLEGAL ALIEN.
LOOK, I KNOW MY FAMILY. SHE'S NOT A PART OF IT, AND I DON'T KNOW WHAT SHE'S AFTER.
THEN WHO IS SHE? WHY KILL AGENT LIBERTY?
I-I DON'T KNOW. I THOUGHT SHE WAS MY FRIEND, BUT...
DO YOU THINK IT'S A COINCIDENCE THAT SHE ENTERED METROPOLIS AIRSPACE A FEW MINUTES AGO, JUST AFTER YOU ARRIVED AT THE POLICE STATION?
WE'VE BEEN TRACKING HER BY SATELLITE. SHE AND HER COMPANION HAVE BEEN FLYING IN A SEARCH PATTERN OVER THE CITY.
WHO'S SHE CARRYING?
I THOUGHT YOU'D RECOGNIZE THE MAN WHO MURDERED YOUR FATHER, SUPERGIRL--
--SHE'S CARRYING REACTRON.
SHE'S... WHAT? SHE'S WORKING WITH HIM?
WHAT DO YOU KNOW ABOUT REACTRON?

I DON'T KNOW MUCH.
BUT IF SUPERWOMAN IS WORKING WITH HIM NOW, IF THEY'RE SEARCHING FOR SOMEONE--
--THEN THEY'LL FIND SOMEONE WAITING.

WHO IS SUPERWOMAN?

PART FOUR: MISTAKES

JAMAL IGLE PENCILS
JON SIBAL INKS

METROPOLIS POLICE PRECINCT #55.
HOME OF THE METROPOLIS METACRIMES DIVISION.
SO WHO DO YOU THINK SHE IS?
I DON'T KNOW. SHE WAS LIVING IN KANDOR WITH THE REST OF US.
KANDOR?
VEE VEE VEE
I'VE GOT TO TAKE THIS.
KANDOR'S OUR CITY, INSPECTOR.
THE CITY THAT BECAME A PLANET. NEW KRYPTON.
YOU LEAD A BIGGER LIFE THAN THE REST OF US, DON'T YOU?
DID YOU KNOW THIS WOMAN IN KANDOR?
I THOUGHT SHE WAS MY FRIEND. NO, MORE THAN A FRIEND. MORE THAN THAT.
THARA AK-VAR.
BUT SHE CAN'T BE SUPERWOMAN.
WHY NOT?

BECAUSE IF SHE IS, THAT MEANS...
...THAT MEANS SHE'S WORKING WITH REACTRON. WHICH MEANS...
...WHICH MEANS MY FRIEND HELPED HIM MURDER MY FATHER IN COLD BLOOD.
YOUR FATHER? I KNEW HE'D BEEN KILLED SOMEHOW, IT WAS ALL OVER THE NEWS, BUT NO ONE SAID HE'D BEEN MURDERED--
WE FOUND SUPERWOMAN.
SATELLITE TRACKED HER DOWNTOWN, THE CORNER OF MALVERNE AND SIEGEL AVE--
THANK YOU, MAJOR LANE.
WOOOSH
NOW, INSPECTOR, LET'S TALK ABOUT NATIONAL SECURITY--
--AND YOU HARBORING AN ILLEGAL ALIEN IN YOUR POLICE STATION.

I FLY FAST.
THARA LIVED WITH MY PARENTS IN THE BOTTLE CITY OF KANDOR. SHE WAS MY FATHER'S CHOICE FOR KANDOR'S SECURITY CHIEF.
IF SHE'S BEEN WORKING WITH REACTRON SINCE KANDOR ARRIVED ON EARTH--
--THEN WHEN WE CAPTURED HIM, SHE LET HIM PASS THROUGH PHANTOM ZONE PROCESSING UNSEARCHED.
I SEARCHED THEM MYSELF. THEY'RE READY.
TAKE THEM DIRECTLY TO THE COURT CHAMBER, COMMANDER GOR.
AND THEN SHE WAS NOWHERE TO BE FOUND WHEN BRAINIAC'S ROBOTS ATTACKED.
SKRAAAACT
AND SO WITH HER ABSENCE AND SEEMING NEGLIGENCE--
--SHE HELPED REACTRON KILL MY FATHER.

AGENT LIBERTY MUST'VE DISCOVERED WHAT SHE'D DONE AND DIED FOR THAT KNOWLEDGE.
SHE'S GOT TO ANSWER FOR HER CRIMES, BOTH HERE--
--AND ON NEW KRYPTON.
THERE.
I HAVE TO MOVE FAST ENOUGH THAT SHE CAN'T POSSIBLY STOP ME.
SO I MOVE FAST. SO SO FAST--

--SO FAST I MAKE A MISTAKE.
KRRRNNNCH
WHAT--?
I DON'T GET IT.
WHY WOULD SHE SET UP A DECOY--

REMEMBER ME, SWEETCHEEKS?!
KRAKK

UUNNH!

GET OFF OF ME!
ALL RIGHT! I HAVEN'T HAD THIS WILD'A RIDE SINCE I WAS IN THE ARMY--
LET GO, YOU SON OF A--
KKRRRRKK
AGGHH!
FINE! YOU DON'T WANNA PLAY NICE?
THEN LET'S PLAY DIRTY!
WRRR
I HEAR THE COMPARTMENT OPEN AND I'M INSTANTLY NAUSEOUS. I'VE FELT THIS BEFORE.
GOLD KRYPTONITE. WHICH TEMPORARILY TAKES AWAY MY--
--POWERS.

FREEFALL--
--I THINK OF MY FATHER'S HAND SLIPPING OUT OF MINE--
--REMEMBER THIS. TRAINING. REMEMBER. NO POWERS--
--MY MOTHER CRADLING HIS BODY IN HER ARMS. I WAS POWERLESS TO SAVE HIM--
"NO POWERS."
--I CAN'T END LIKE THIS--
"NO POWERS."
BATMAN TOLD ME...
YOU HAVE FORMIDABLE NATURAL KRYPTONIAN ABILITIES, YES, BUT YOU WILL FIGHT OPPONENTS THAT CAN DRAIN THEM, DISTORT THEM, OR EVEN STEAL THEM OUTRIGHT.
IF YOU FIND YOURSELF WITHOUT YOUR POWERS--
"--KNOW HOW TO COMPENSATE AND FIGHT BACK WITH WHAT YOU HAVE ON HAND."
PLEASELETTHISWORK
PLEASELETTHISWORK
PLEASELETTHISWORK

THANKYOURAOTHANK YOURAOTHANKYOURAO
CAN'T...KEEP...
...THIS UP...
...MUCH...LONGER--
NNH--!
NOT THE GREATEST LANDING, BUT...

FIFTEEN SECONDS. GOLD K EFFECT LASTS FIFTEEN SECONDS.
MY POWERS SHOULD BE BACK ANY SECOND--
KOOM
HOPE YOU'RE NOT TOO TIRED FROM YOUR FLIGHT!
SKRACTT
HNNH!

METROPOLIS PUBLIC SCHOOLS
Student Journalism Awards Banquet
7:30-9:30
AWARDS PRESENTED BY MEMBERS OF THE...
DAILY PLANET
CAT GRANT
LANA LANG
JAMES OLSEN
LANA.
CAT. NICE DRESS, BY THE WAY.
HMPH. USELESS DRESS, YOU MEAN.
DON'T ANY OF THESE KIDS HAVE SINGLE RICH FATHERS?
HOW LONG DID PERRY SAY WE HAD TO BE HERE? AND WHAT BOY TOY DO YOU KEEP SNEAKING AWAY TO CALL?
WE STAY UNTIL IT'S OVER. IT'S GOOD P.R.
AND I'VE BEEN TRYING TO CALL MY NIECE. SHE HAD A...THING TONIGHT, AND I STILL HAVEN'T HEARD BACK FROM HER.
YES, I SAW YOU PARADING HER AROUND THE OFFICE. DIDN'T LOOK LIKE MUCH OF A WILD CHILD TO ME.
--USED TO DRIVE A MOTORCYCLE, BUT I CRASHED IT TO GET AWAY FROM THIS TELEPATHIC SUPER-VILLAIN--
A SUPER-VILLAIN? THAT'S SOOOOO COOL!
YOU'LL LEARN, YOU RUN FROM 'EM ALL THE TIME IN THIS BUSINESS. ANYWAY, HE WAS CHASING ME ACROSS THE DESERT, AND--
I WORRY ABOUT HER SOMETIMES. HER HOME LIFE'S BEEN A WRECK SINCE HER FATHER PASSED AWAY, SO SHE'S BEEN STAYING WITH ME--
BROTHER OR SISTER?
EXCUSE ME?
SHE'S YOUR NIECE, RIGHT? SO IS SHE YOUR BROTHER'S CHILD, OR YOUR SIS--
HOLY--! LOOK AT THAT!
OH, WOW. WHAT DO YOU THINK THAT IS, GUYS?
I-I DON'T KNOW, JIMMY, BUT WHATEVER IT IS--

"--IT DOESN'T LOOK GOOD."
SKRAKHOOOM
NAAH--!
I LIED TO YOU THE FIRST TIME WE MET, SUPERGIRL. THAT "STARSUIT" I WAS WEARING?
IT DIDN'T PROJECT MY CONSCIOUSNESS INTO ANOTHER PART OF THE GALAXY OR ANY OF THAT BULL. GUESS I THOUGHT I WAS BEING FUNNY.
TRUTH IS, I WAS A SICK MAN. DYING OF A RADIATION POISONING THE SCIENCE GEEKS HAD NEVER SEEN BEFORE.
THAT "STARSUIT" WAS GOING TO HEAL ME COMPLETELY. SAVE MY ROTTEN LIFE.
BUT YOU DESTROYED IT, ALONG WITH MY CHANCE AT RECOVERY. MADE THE PAIN EVEN WORSE.
LUCKILY, SOMEONE FOUND A DIFFERENT WAY TO SAVE MY LIFE.
THEY GAVE ME A NEW TOY TO PLAY WITH. THIS LITTLE ROCK CHANGED ME. CONNECTED ME TO YOU.
GAVE ME A CHANCE TO GET BACK AT YOU FOR WHAT YOU DID TO ME.
AND LEMME TELL YOU--
--IT FELT SO GOOD PUTTING THAT HOLE IN YOUR DADDY'S CHES--

WNNG
SHUT--
--UP!
HRRK!
CGHCGH... NOT...BAD... WHERE'D...?
I TRAINED WITH BATMAN. WITH THE AMAZONS. I KNOW FIRST LEVEL
JUST BECAUSE I CAN'T USE HEAT VISION DOESN'T MEAN I'M HELP-LESS.

YOU LIKE HAND-TO-HAND?
SKRACTT
HOW 'BOUT HAND-TO-FACE?
THIS CLOSE...SICK... HIS POWER...
HE KEPT TALKING...ABOUT... THE KRYPTONITE, ITS...CONNECTION.
SO WHAT HAPPENS...
...IF I BREAK THAT CONNECTION?
WHAT? N-NO!
STOP!

AAAAAHHH!
GIVE IT BACK! GIVE IT!
FSSS
NNGH!
NO!
REACTRON--

HE'S...
...GONE. HOW--?
IT DOESN'T MATTER. HE'S ESCAPED AND I'VE FAILED MY MOTHER AGAIN.
AND MY FATHER.
BUT I'M ALIVE. I'LL FIND HIM AGAIN.
MY POWERS ARE RETURNING. I CAN FEEL MY BODY HEALING THE BRUISES AND CUTS.
MY BRAIN SPEEDS BACK UP. THE NAUSEA PASSES.
I CAN SEE EVERYTHING AGAIN.
I CAN SEE...I SEE SOMETHING THAT I HADN'T SEEN BEFORE...
I'VE MADE ANOTHER MISTAKE.
I KNOW WHO SUPERWOMAN IS.
AND WHERE SHE'S GOING NEXT.

WHAT DID I THINK? I THOUGHT SHE COULD HELP ME SOLVE A MURDER, BILL!
BILL, THAT'S RIDICULOUS!
I'VE WORKED HARD TO MAKE THIS UNIT A REALITY! YOU CAN'T JUST TAKE IT--
--AWAY...
NO, I DID NOT THINK I WAS ENDANGERING NATIONAL SECURITY--
NO, OF COURSE SHE DIDN'T! SHE'S SUPERMAN'S COUSIN, BILL! LOOK, YOU'RE THE COMMISSIONER, CAN'T YOU--
SO LONG! AND KEEP REPORTING!
I THOUGHT YOU WERE INTERESTED IN GIRLS YOUR OWN AGE, RED.
OH, THEY'RE JUST EXCITED TO BE ENTERING THE FIELD, MS. GRANT. I REMEMBER WHEN I FIRST DECLARED MYSELF A CUB REPORTER--
MS. LANG? YOU OKAY?
I'M FINE...
JUST A LITTLE... WOOZY...
"LET ME CALL YOU BACK."

HELLO?
SUPERGIRL?
MS. LANG!
MS. GRANT, SEE IF THERE'S A DOCTOR BACK THERE!
SOMEONE CALL AN AMBULANCE!
"IT'S AN EMERGENCY!"
YOU--

HNNGH--!
VZZT
YOU MIGHT WANT TO ALERT YOUR MEN--
--THERE'S AN INTRUDER IN YOUR OFF--

YOU LIED TO ME!
YOU'VE BEEN TRYING TO GET CLOSE TO ME FOR WEEKS!
TRYING TO WEASEL YOUR WAY IN! SMILING AT ME!
PRETENDING TO BE MY FRIEND WHEN YOU HELPED KILL MY FATHER!
WHY DID YOU DO IT?
NNNGQUIT!
TELL ME WHY YOU DID IT--

--MAJOR LANE!

WHO IS SUPERWOMAN?

PART FIVE: DAUGHTERS OF KRYPTON

FERNANDO DAGNINO PENCILS
RAÚL FERNANDEZ INKS

METROPOLIS.
ELLSWORTH MEMORIAL HOSPITAL.
DOCTOR, IS SHE GOING TO BE OKAY?
WE WON'T KNOW ANYTHING UNTIL WE RUN SOME TESTS, MISS. NOW, PLEASE GO BACK OUT TO THE WAITING ROOM!
BUT WHAT IF SHE REGAINS CONSCIOUSNESS? SHE'LL WANT SOMEONE THERE--
ARE EITHER OF YOU THE PATIENT'S FAMILY?
NO, WE'RE NOT, BUT--
THEN I'M SORRY, I CAN'T LET YOU GO ANY FARTHER. PLEASE PROCEED TO THE WAITING ROOM.
ONCE WE HAVE A BETTER IDEA OF WHAT'S HAPPENING, WE'LL COME FIND YOU.
YOU THINK MS. LANG WILL BE ALL RIGHT, MS. GRANT?
I DON'T KNOW, RED.
I DON'T KNOW.

PROJECT 7734
THIS HAD BETTER BE IMPORTANT.
TRACK_ACTIVE
ALPHA 398
SUBJECT_SUPERWOMAN
IT IS, SIR.
WHAT AM I LOOKING AT, LIEUTENANT?
CAMERA FEEDS FROM DOWNTOWN METROPOLIS, SIR. SOME FROM OUR CAMERAS, OTHERS FROM AREA INCIDENTALS.
SUPERWOMAN?

CO-OPT OR JAM EVERY CAMERA IN THE AREA, FROM THE STREET LEVEL UP.
TRAFFIC CAMERAS, STORE SECURITY CAMERAS, CELL PHONES, EVERYTHING. SATELLITE FEEDS, TOO.
I DON'T WANT ANYONE TO SEE THIS OR HAVE A RECORD OF IT.
TRACK_ACTIVE
ALPHA 398
SUBJECT_SUPERWOMAN
REACTRON?
HER IDENTITY'S BEEN COMPROMISED, SIR.
BY SUPERGIRL.
ON SCENE, SIR, AND CAN STRIKE AS SOON AS HE'S AUTHORIZED.
GOOD.
ADVISE HIM TO STAND BY. AND KEY IN TO MAJOR LANE'S COMMUNICATOR. I WANT TO HEAR EVERYTHING.
LET'S SEE IF MAJOR LANE CAN CLEAN UP AFTER HERSELF.

MY THOUGHTS REEL AND TUMBLE AND TRY TO MAKE SENSE OF THEMSELVES.
WEEKS AGO, DURING AN ATTACK ON KANDOR, MY FATHER WAS MURDERED BY A MAN NAMED REACTRON.
SOMEONE HELPED REACTRON ESCAPE US AFTERWARDS. HELPED HIM DISAPPEAR.
TELL ME WHY, MAJOR LANE!
WHICH, IN A CITY FULL OF PEOPLE WITH SUPER-SENSES, IS NO EASY FEAT.
--SOMEONE FIRED TWO MORE BEAMS INTO THE CHEST OF INSPECTOR MIKE HENDERSON OF THE METROPOLIS METACRIMES DIVISION.
THE MAN WHO WAS INVESTIGATING AGENT LIBERTY'S MURDER.
MY COUSIN'S

RECENTLY, A PAIR OF HEAT VISION BEAMS TO THE HEAD KILLED A SUPERHERO NAMED AGENT LIBERTY.
SECONDS AGO, WHILE I WAS BUSY BEING PLAYED BY REACTRON ON A ROOFTOP--
I HAVE MY REASONS.
LUCY LANE.
NO, NOT LUCY LANE. NOT ANYMORE.
NOW, SUPERWOMAN.
WHICH MEANS--
--WHICH MEANS--

--WHICH MEANS SOMEONE IN MY FAMILY HELPED KILL MY FATHER.
REASONS?!
I WANT TO THROW UP.
WHAT'S WRONG WITH YOU? WHAT REASONS COULD EXCUSE WHAT YOU'VE DONE?
IT REALLY DOESN'T MATTER, DOES IT? YOU WANT ANSWERS, BUT I'M NOT GOING TO GIVE YOU ANY.
WERE YOU--DID YOU--
--DID YOU HELP REACTRON KILL MY FATHER? HELP HIM ESCAPE?
AND THEN LIE TO ME AND CLAIM TO BE MY FRIEND?
AND LIKE THE LITTLE GIRL YOU ARE, YOU ASSUME THIS WAS ALL ABOUT YOU.
IT'S NOT.
I TOLD YOU BEFORE. IT'S ABOUT THIS.

THAT DOESN'T ANSWER MY QUESTION.
AND HOW ARE YOU DUPLICATING KRYPTONIAN ABILITIES? EVEN YOUR DNA LOOKS KRYPTONIAN--
SHE DOESN'T--SHE CAN'T KNOW THAT KAL AND CLARK KENT ARE THE SAME PERSON. SHE DOESN'T KNOW WHO SHE'S HURTING.
NOT ALL MYSTERIES ARE MEANT TO BE EASILY SOLVED, KARA.
KNOW THAT YOUR MOTHER'S MISSION FOR YOU CHANGED MY OWN. GOOD OPERATIONS REQUIRE IMPROVISATION.
NOW THAT YOU'RE HERE ON EARTH--
--SOMEONE ELSE CAN PLAY THE ROLE OF AGENT LIBERTY'S KRYPTONIAN MURDERER.
BUT THE HARD DRIVE IMAGE--
"WAS EASILY DEALT WITH, ALONG WITH RECORDS OF ITS EXISTENCE.
"AND WITH THE GOOD INSPECTOR COUNTING FEATHERS ON HIS WINGS IN HEAVEN--"
--NO ONE WILL BE ABLE TO POINT THE FINGER AT ME.
I'LL MAKE SURE THAT YOU ARE THE ONE WHO'S BLAMED.
UNFORTUNATELY FOR YOU, YOU WON'T BE ABLE TO TELL THEM OTHERWISE--

--AS YOU'LL HAVE SUFFERED A "MYSTERIOUS DISAPPEARANCE."
UNNH--!
MMM.
MUCH, MUCH BETTER.
AND DON'T BOTHER TRYING TO PUT UP A FIGHT, GIRL.
I'M JUST AS INVULNERABLE AS YOU ARE.
GOOD.
THAT MEANS I WON'T HAVE TO HOLD BACK, YOU MURDEROUS

KRAAKK
AWESOME!
ARE YOU SEEING THIS!?
HEY--!
KRRNGK

BEAT IT.
IT'S THE ATOMIC SKULL! RUN!
HNH.
REACTRON TO BASE.
GO AHEAD, MAJOR KRULL.
"I'VE GOT A VISUAL ON THE SUPER-LADIES."
HOW LONG HAVE YOU BEEN WATCHING ME?
WHAT WERE YOU DOING ON NEW KRYPTON?!
TELL ME!
CHOOM
YOU SHOULDN'T ≥NNN≤ WORRY ABOUT THAT...
I'D WORRY... ≥NNN≤ ABOUT SOMEONE SEEING YOU AT THE SCENE OF ANOTHER M-M--
--MURDER--
KKKRRRRKKK

METROPOLIS POLICE PRECINCT #55.
NINTH FLOOR.
VROOOMMMMMM
CGHCGH
SHE'S RIGHT.
I'VE GOT TO GET US BOTH OUT OF HERE. AWAY FROM THE EYES OF METROPOLIS.
WING CLOSED FOR RENOVATIONS
MAYBE I SHOULD TAKE HER TO THE FORTRESS--
--OR EVEN SPACE--
NO.
...N-NOT AGAIN...
Y'KNOW, EVER SINCE I WAS IN HIGH SCHOOL--

--I'VE REALLY GOTTEN A KICK OUT OF CRASHING OTHER PEOPLE'S PARTIES.
GOLD KRYPTONITE. F-F-FIFTEEN SECONDS--
--FIFTEEN SECONDS UNTIL I CAN FIGHT BACK.
I THINK YOU DROPPED THIS. STILL NEED A HAND?
WRRR
STAY AWAY FROM ME, KRULL.
ALL RIGHT, FINE. DON'T GET YOUR CAPE INNA BUNCH. JUST TRYING TO HEL--
NOBODY MOVE!
OH, GOODY.
THE OTHER PARTY GUESTS HAVE ARRIVED.
KEEP YOUR HANDS WHERE I CAN SEE 'EM.
FOURTEEN SECONDS... THIRTEEN...
YOU TAKE THEM--
--I'LL DEAL WITH HER.
YOU GUYS EVER SEE THAT MOVIE "THE TERMINATOR"? LEMME TELL YA ABOUT MY FAVORITE SCENE.
"YOU HAVE ALL FAILED--"

--SO DECLARED THE MYSTERIOUS MAN KNOWN AS THE OLYMPIAN TODAY TO THE UNITED NATIONS ASSEMBLY.
OLYMPIAN INVADES UN
ERO KNOWN AS MON-EL IN METROPOLIS TO
THE OLYMPIAN'S EXTREME DEMONSTRATION COMES CLOSE ON THE HEELS OF THE UN'S DECLARATION BANNING ALL KRYPTONIANS FROM THE PLANET EARTH, SAVE FOR SUPERMAN--
X RAY
HEY, GUYS.
LANA?
SORRY YOU HAD TO WAIT ON ME. I'M HEADING HOME.
UM, THEY DON'T WANT TO KEEP YOU OVERNIGHT, MS. LANG? YOU LOOKED PRETTY BAD--
THEY SAID THEY'LL HAVE TO RUN MORE TESTS EVENTUALLY, BUT THEY'VE RELEASED ME FOR THE NIGHT.
WELL, THAT DOESN'T SEEM RIGHT, LANA. DO THEY HAVE ANY IDEA WHAT CAUSED YOU TO--
LOOK, I'M TIRED, CAT. I WANT TO GO HOME AND TAKE A BATH AND GO TO SLEEP.
THANK YOU FOR STAYING-- I APPRECIATE IT, I REALLY DO--BUT I'LL JUST SEE YOU BOTH MONDAY MORNING.
OH, AND PLEASE KEEP THIS TO YOURSELF. I DON'T NEED PERRY AND HALF THE PLANET STAFF WORRYING ABOUT ME.
YOU, UH, GOT IT, MS. LANG. YOU SURE YOU DON'T NEED HELP GETTING HOME?
NO, THANKS, JIMMY. HAVE A GREAT WEEKEND.
IN OTHER NEWS, PREMIERING SOON IS OUR NEWEST PROGRAM, "THE EDGE OF REASON," HOSTED BY MORGAN EDGE. WE'LL HAVE MR. EDGE ON THE SHOW TOMORROW TO DISCUSS--

CHNNG
AAIIHGGGGGGUL!
NO HARD FEELINGS, PAL.
HSSS
BLAM
BLAM
FFSSSSSSS
...S-SEVEN SECONDS...
LET'S MOVE THIS ALONG.
NNG.
KRKK
I THINK I OVERCOOKED THE BACON.
SUPERTEEN STILL POWER-LESS?
OR DOES SHE NEED ANOTHER BLAST OF GOLD KRYPTONITE?
I HEARD...ONLY THING THAT STOPS KRYPTONITE IS... LEAD...
YOU--
...JUST GOTTA KNOW...WHERE TO PUT IT...
FOUR SECONDS.

NNNRRRRH!
BLAM
THREE SECONDS.
KRULL, WATCH OUT!

WATCH--
FFSSSSSSS
ONE.

NYAIEEEE!
TIME'S UP.
IS THAT HOW YOU DID IT?! WHY YOU LOOK KRYPTONIAN?
IT'S THOSE DISCS!?

SUBJECT UNCONCIOUS
REACTRON'S LOST CONSCIOUSNESS, SIR.
I'M NOT WORRIED ABOUT MAJOR KRULL, SERGEANT, WE'LL FETCH HIM LATER. ARE WE STILL TRACKING MAJOR LANE?
YES, SIR. THEY'RE MOVING NORTH AT HIGH SPEEDS, AND WE'RE GETTING MASSIVE ENERGY SPIKES FROM SUPERWOMAN'S SUIT--
SUIT POWERING DOWN
MAJOR LANE'S A PROFESSIONAL, GENTLEMEN.
"SHE WON'T LET THAT TEENAGE HUSSY GET THE BETTER OF HER."
GET YOUR HANDS OFF ME! AND IT'S NOT THE DISCS, YOU STUPID--
VZZT
NO? SO WHAT HAPPENS RRRR WHEN THEY COME--
--OFF!
HKKKKGG!
YOU'VE GOT TO STOP, KARA!
STOP? I HAVEN'T EVEN STARTED!
SIR? THE CONTAINMENT FIELD IS PITCHING WAY OUT OF CONTROL. IF WE'RE GOING TO HELP--
I RAISED A SOLDIER, MR. BENNETT. SHE'LL BE FINE.
SUPER-- KARA!
STOP! PLEASE!
YOU DON'T KNOW WHAT YOU'RE DOING!

YOU'RE ASKING FOR MERCY?
LIKE AGENT LIBERTY GOT?!
LIKE POOR MISTER HENDERSON!?
LIKE MY FATHER!?
YOU DON'T DESERVE MERCY, YOU DESERVE A BEATING!
AND THIS?
YOU DON'T DESERVE TO WEAR THIS.
SHRRPPP
AAAAAAH!!

HHHRRRRRHH!
--S-S-STUPID GIRL!
-YOU DON'T--KNOW--WASN'T THE DISCS--
NNNGGG!
--SUIT--H-H-HURTS--
THE SUIT HURTS?
SUPERWOM--
LUCY! WHAT CAN I DO TO HELP--
--G-GET AWAY--
--NNNNKILLED ME--
--YOU'VE KILLED MUH--
--MUH--
ME.

SKABOOM
SUBJECT DECEASED
SUIT DESTROYED
SUBJECT DECEASED
SUIT DESTROYED
NO.

CHOOOOOOM
OFFICER DOWN! NINTH FLOOR!
I WOULDN'T TOUCH HIM--
METAHOSTILE'S GOT A PULSE, TOO!
HIS PULSE IS STEADY.
SIR, WHAT DO WE DO NOW?
SIR?
...SIR?

I--
--THE SUIT--
--I COULDN'T--
--DID I--
--DID I JUST--
--DID I JUST KILL LOIS'S SISTER?

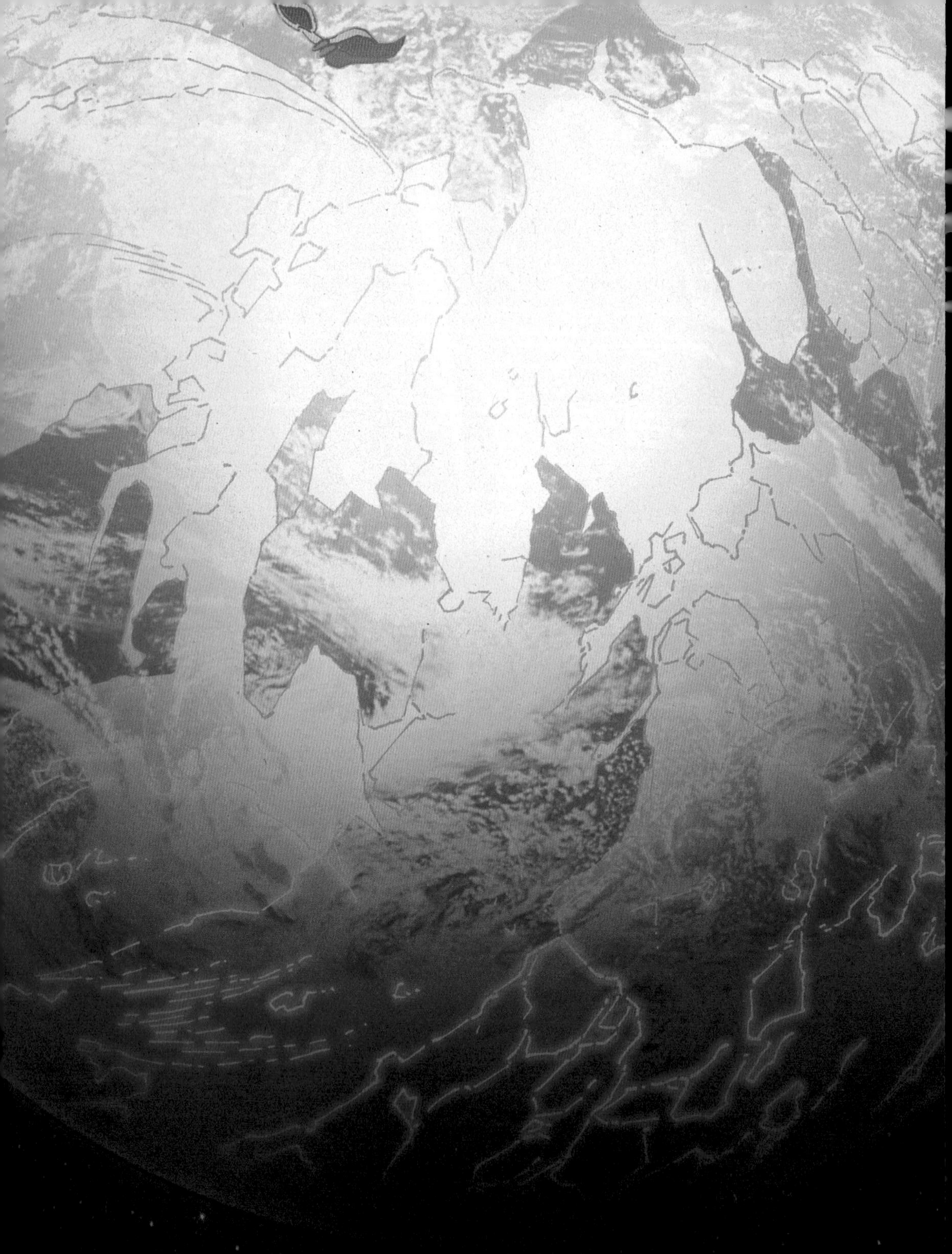

WHO IS SUPERWOMAN?

CONCLUSION: EPILOGUES & HOMECOMINGS

JAMAL IGLE PENCILS

JON SIBAL INKS

MT. KATAHDIN.
PISCATAQUIS COUNTY, MAINE.
US ARMY
GENERAL SAM LANE IS NOT A MAN WHO LETS HIS FEELINGS SHOW IN FRONT OF THE MEN AND WOMEN IN HIS COMMAND.
HE REMEMBERS. YEARS AGO, HE WORKED UNDER A SERGEANT WHOSE VISAGE WAS AS HARD AS A ROCK. A GREAT MAN. THAT MAN WARNED HIM:
"IT AIN'T EASY BEIN' IN CHARGE OF OTHERS, LANE. BEIN' THE TOP-KICKER IS TOUGH.
"IF YOU LOSE ONE OF YOUR MEN IN THE FIELD, THOUGH, DON'T YOU SHED A TEAR. NOT EVEN IF THEY'RE YER OWN BROTHER.
"ENEMIES SEE THOSE TEARS, LANE, AND IT'LL JUST GIVE 'EM SOMETHING SHINY TO AIM AT."
SINCE THEN, GENERAL LANE HASN'T CRIED. NOT ONCE.
NOT WHEN HIS DAUGHTER LOIS MARRIED THAT OAF OF A MAN, CLARK KENT.
NOT EVEN WHEN HE FAKED HIS OWN DEATH AND SEVERED ALL TIES TO HIS FAMILY.
NOT EVEN THIS MORNING.

HE REMEMBERS...
--BE IN DEEP UNDERCOVER. REMEMBER, THE SUIT IS TETHERED TO YOU.
AS LONG AS YOU'RE WITHIN RANGE OF ITS FIELD, YOU'LL APPEAR TO BE KRYPTONIAN TO THEM.
YOU'LL HAVE NO BACKUP OF ANY KIND ON THAT PLANET, MAJOR.
IF YOU'RE DISCOVERED, THERE'S NO TELLING WHAT THE KRYPTONIANS MIGHT DO TO A SPY.
NEW KRYPTON-ANTIPODAL ORBIT ESTABLISHED.
ARE YOU WILLING TO DIE FOR YOUR COUNTRY--NO.
ARE YOU WILLING TO DIE FOR YOUR PLANET, MAJOR?
S-SIR?
LISTEN. I KNOW WHO YOU ARE. DEEP DOWN INSIDE.
DON'T BE SCARED.
YOU'RE MY DAUGHTER. YOU'RE GOING TO FOLLOW YOUR ORDERS WITH THE UTMOST BRAVERY.
AND YOU'RE GOING TO MAKE ME VERY, VERY PROUD.
GENERAL LANE?

DREW.
WE'VE GONE OVER THE AREA SIX TIMES, SIR. WE'VE FOUND TINY BITS OF FLESH AND HAIR THAT MATCH HER DNA, BUT...
...NOTHING SUBSTANTIAL.
OF COURSE NOT. IF SUPERGIRL DISRUPTED THE FIELD, THE SUIT WOULD'VE OVERCOMPENSATED.
IT WOULD'VE PRACTICALLY VAPORIZED HER.
NO, I'M AFRAID MAJOR LANE'S NOTHING MORE THAN...
SSSSSS
LANE
WE'RE NOT GOING TO JUST KILL HER, DREW.
SIR?
SHE KILLED A LANE TODAY. NO, WE'RE NOT GOING TO JUST KILL HER.
I'VE GOT SOMETHING IN MIND THAT'S FAR, FAR WORSE.

METROPOLIS.
THE NEXT DAY.
I TOLD LOIS EVERYTHING.
...AND THAT'S WHAT HAPPENED.

EVERYTHING.

LOIS?
I DIDN'T AT FIRST. I'D ONLY MET LUCY ONCE BEFORE THAT NIGHT AT THE POLICE STATION.
WHEN SUPERWOMAN FIRST APPROACHED ME, I TRIED TO SEE HER FACE--
"--BUT THE SUIT INTERFERED WITH MY VISION."
IS THAT LEAD?
HER WHOLE SUIT WAS LIKE THAT. I COULDN'T TELL WHAT IT WAS MADE OF WHEN I LOOKED AT IT. AND I COULDN'T SEE THROUGH IT.
"--AND I REMEMBERED SOMETHING ELSE.
"MAJOR LANE'S CELL PHONE. WHEN IT RANG, I KNEW I'D HEARD THAT SOUND BEFORE.
"BUT IT WASN'T A CELL PHONE I WAS HEARING. IT WAS SUPERWOMAN'S COMMUNICATOR."
VEE VEE VEE
I'VE GOT TO TAKE THIS.
HOW DID YOU--?

EXPLAIN IT TO ME AGAIN.
WHAT?
EXPLAIN IT TO ME AGAIN, KARA. HOW YOU KNEW SUPERWOMAN WAS MY SISTER.
"AND THEN A PIECE OF IT WAS SEPARATED FROM THE REST, AND WHATEVER WAS CAUSING IT TO INTERFERE WITH MY VISION WAS GONE.
"I COULD SEE IT FOR WHAT IT WAS: REGULAR FABRIC.
"FABRIC WITH BITS AND PIECES OF HUMAN HAIR AND SKIN ALL OVER IT.
"AND THAT GOT ME THINKING--
I'D HEARD IT WHEN WE FIRST FOUGHT. WHEN I WAS HALF UNCONSCIOUS. THE EXACT SAME SOUND.
I JUST DIDN'T PUT IT TOGETHER AT THE POLICE STATION, AND MAJOR LANE PLAYED IT OFF.
THEN I--I CONFRONTED HER AND PULLED OFF THAT MASK SO FAST SHE COULDN'T STOP ME, AND--
--AND--
--IT WAS HER, LOIS. YOUR SISTER.
YOU'RE SURE?

YOU'RE POSITIVE IT WAS HER. IT WASN'T PARASITE POSING AS HER, OR A WHITE MARTIAN, OR A ROBOT, OR...
...OR...
LOIS, WHEN WAS THE LAST TIME YOU SAW LUCY--
KARA, I NEED YOU TO LEAVE.
WHAT?
I NEED YOU TO LEAVE RIGHT NOW.
WHAT? WHY?
LOIS, SHE WAS WORKING WITH THE MAN WHO KILLED MY DAD. I'M SORRY, BUT--

I UNDERSTAND YOU'RE SORRY. I'M SORRY THIS PERSON WAS HELPING REACTRON.
BUT I NEED PROOF, AND WHAT YOU'RE TELLING ME ISN'T ENOUGH.
I JUST THINK IT'S IN EVERYONE'S BEST INTERESTS IF YOU LEAVE.
NOW.
LOIS, DID YOU KNOW LUCY WAS--
THE LAST TIME I SAW HER WAS AFTER JONATHAN'S FUNERAL.
TO ANSWER YOU.
AT DAD'S GRAVE IN WASHINGTON. SHE SAID...SHE SAID SHE WAS TRYING TO MAKE OUR FATHER PROUD OF HER.
TRYING TO LIVE UP TO WHAT HE WOULD EXPECT OF HER.
SERIOUSLY, KARA, I NEED YOU OUT OF THIS APARTMENT.
C'MON, HONEY. LET'S GO--
I DIDN'T DO ANYTHING WRONG, LOIS! SHE WAS TRYING TO KILL ME!
I KNOW, KARA. BUT LET'S DO WHAT LOIS IS ASKING.
WAIT.

LEAVE ME A PIECE OF THE COSTUME.
I'M GOING TO HAVE SOME PEOPLE LOOK AT IT.
VZZT

I'M--
--I'M SORRY, LOIS.
I KNOW, KARA. I KNOW YOU ARE.
BUT I DON'T WANT TO SEE YOU RIGHT NOW.
YES, I'D LIKE TO BOOK A TICKET.
METROPOLIS TO WASHINGTON NATIONAL.

ELSEWHERE.
WHO IS THIS REACTRON GUY, ANYWAY?
YOU REALLY DON'T PAY ATTENTION DURING BRIEFINGS, DO YOU, GARRISON?
SUE ME, COOK. UPSTAIRS NEIGHBOR'S GOT A THREE-YEAR- OLD AND A ONE-YEAR-OLD. I SLEEP HALF AN HOUR A NIGHT. I STEAL WHAT Z'S I CAN.
UNFORTUNATELY, I HAPPENED TO CATCH SOME THIS MORNING WHEN WE GOT THIS ASSIGNMENT.
HARPER FINDS YOU SLEEPING THROUGH CLASS AGAIN, GARRISON--
--AND HE'LL DO WORSE THAN SEND YOU TO THE PRINCIPAL.
THIS REACTRON GUY'S THE WORST KIND OF CRIMINAL: A COP KILLER.
SMASHED HIS WAY INTO PRECINCT FIVE FIVE AND KILLED A BUNCH OF UNIS BEFORE ANYONE COULD STOP HIM.
GUY WHO TOOK HIM DOWN GOT HURT, STILL HASN'T WOKEN UP. NOT SURE HE WILL.
SO STAY FROSTY AND LET'S GET THIS JOB DONE. YOU CAN NAP ON THE WAY HOME.
IT'S A PRISONER TRANSPO AND WE'RE ALL WEARING BATTLE SUITS, WILCOX--
--WHAT'S THE WORST THAT COULD HAPPEN?
STAR
THESE S.T.A.R. EGGHEADS ARE EXPECTING US, RIGHT?
YEAH.
SO WHERE ARE--
PARKER
GARRISON
WILCOX

SURPRISE, NERDS!
GOOD GOD!
AIIEEE!
KZZZAKK
CONTROL! SCIPO GROUP #742, REQUESTING BACKUP AT S.T.A.R. LABS!
WE'VE GOT METAHOSTILES AND MEN DOWN!
CONTROL! ARE YOU READING ME?!
WE NEED BACKUP RIGHT NOW--
REPEAT, MEN DOWN AHHH!

...RIGHT NOW AT...
...S.T.A.R. LABS...
...WHERE'S... BACKUP...?
NO, MR. SAVAGE... I HATE TO TANGO...
WILCOX
deet
HELLO, MAJOR KRULL.
SSSSSS
HHHNNNHH

UNNNH.
TH-THANK YOU FOR THE "GET OUT OF JAIL" CARD, COLONEL.
THANK THE GENERAL.
WHAT'D YOU DO--?
SOMETHING R&D ASKED ME TO TEST.
LOW-GRADE NONLETHAL PSYCHIC GRENADE.
AMPLIFIES MY ABILITIES AND PRODUCES WAKING NIGHTMARES IN VICTIMS. COMPLETELY INCAPACITATING.
THEY'LL WAKE UP IN HALF AN HOUR WITH A HEADACHE AND A LOT OF QUESTIONS THEY CAN'T ANSWER.
AND IF YOUR TOY HADN'T WORKED?
THEN I WOULD'VE LIVED UP TO MY CODENAME.
LET'S CUT THE SMALL TALK AND MOVE AT DOUBLE TIME, MAJOR. ACTUALLY...
...MAYBE THIS WILL PUT A LITTLE FIRE BACK INTO YOU.
CONSIDER ME HOT TO THE TOUCH, SIR.
"THE MANHUNT BEGAN FOR THE VILLAIN KNOWN AS REACTRON EARLIER TODAY--"

--AFTER HE MYSTERIOUSLY ESCAPED SCIENCE POLICE CUSTODY.
METROPOLIS SCIENCE POLICE FIELD COMMANDER JIM HARPER VOWED THAT REACTRON WOULD IMMEDIATELY BE CAUGHT AND HELD ACCOUNTABLE FOR HIS CRIMES.
TODAY JUST SUCKS.
I THINK TODAY WENT AS WELL AS COULD BE EXPECTED, REALLY.
I WISH I COULD'VE STOPPED REACTRON FROM KILLING THOSE POLICEMEN.
THEY DIDN'T DESERVE TO DIE THAT WAY.
AS FOR SUPERWOMAN...
LANA, YOU KNOW THERE WAS NOTHING I COULD'VE DONE, RIGHT? THE SUIT, IT--
--SHE EXPLODED. I COULDN'T HAVE KNOWN THAT WAS GOING TO HAPPEN.
SOMETHING WAS CLEARLY WRONG WITH LUCY.
I THINK THE BIGGER QUESTION IS--
--WHO WAS HELPING HER? THERE'S NO CONCEIVABLE WAY SHE COULD HAVE MADE THAT SUIT BY HERSELF.
DID YOU KNOW HER?

NEW YORK
LANE
D.C. 2000
Rebate Center
P.O. Box 112119
Central City, WI
LUCILLE LANE
PRSRT STD PAID
PENNYS
I'D MET HER A FEW TIMES. ONCE AT LOIS AND CLARK'S WEDDING.
SHE ALWAYS SEEMED SO DESPERATE TO PROVE HERSELF TO EVERYONE.
"I JUST ASSUMED IT WAS BECAUSE SHE WAS LOIS'S YOUNGER SISTER.
"IT WASN'T EASY FOR THOSE GIRLS, GROWING UP IN A MILITARY HOUSEHOLD.
"LOIS ALWAYS PAINTED THIER FATHER IN A BAD LIGHT. TOO BUSY WITH HIS CAREER TO CARE FOR THEM.
"HE DIED FIGHTING OFF AN ALIEN INVASION A FEW YEARS BACK.
"LUCY WAS DISTRAUGHT.
"SHE AND LOIS HAD A HUGE FALLING OUT.
"LOIS KIND OF LOST TRACK OF HER AFTER THAT--

"--AND I DON'T THINK THEIR RELATIONSHIP EVER RECOVERED."
SO YOU'RE REALLY GOING BACK?
I HAVE TO.
DID YOU SEE INSPECTOR HENDERSON--
YEAH.
Thank you for everything, Inspector. I owe you.
"I ALREADY WENT BY."

WHAT ARE YOU GOING TO TELL YOUR MOTHER ABOUT REACTRON?
I'LL TELL HER THE TRUTH.
I'LL TELL HER EVERYTHING.
BUT WITH ALL THAT'S HAPPENED, I'VE GOT TO GO BACK. SUPERWOMAN WAS LIVING IN OUR CITY.
SHE HAD TO HAVE KEPT AN APARTMENT. SOMETHING. I'VE GOT TO LOOK INTO IT BEFORE THE TRAIL GOES COLD.
KARA, TAKE CARE OF YOURSELF OVER THERE. AND DON'T LET YOUR MOTHER PUSH YOU AROUND.
DON'T FORGET.
YOU'RE SUPERGIRL. STRONGEST GIRL ON THE PLANET.
PFFT MORE LIKE BOTH PLANETS.
HA. DON'T PUSH YOUR LUCK, KIDDO.
I'LL CALL LOIS TOMORROW, MAKE SURE SHE'S OKAY.
THANK YOU, LANA. FOR EVERYTHING.
YOU'RE WELCOME, KAR--
Y'KNOW WHAT?

WHEN I'M HERE, WHY DON'T YOU JUST CALL ME LINDA FROM NOW ON?
ARE YOU SURE?
ABSOLUTELY.
IN THAT CASE--
--SO LONG, LINDA LANG.
SEE YOU SOON, LANA LANG.
AND DON'T FORGET TO FEED MY CAT!
WHOOOOOOOSH
dedeet dedeet
HELLO?
MISS LANG? DR. CODY, FROM ELLSWORTH MEMORIAL. WE'VE GOTTEN YOUR TEST RESULTS BACK, MA'AM.
AND?
MISS LANG, I DON'T KNOW WHAT TO SAY, OTHER THAN--

"I'M SORRY."
THAT'S WHAT I HAVE TO OPEN WITH.
"I'M SORRY, MOTHER."
SHE'S NOT GOING TO LIKE WHAT I HAVE TO SAY TO HER.
BUT I CAN'T KEEP LETTING HER USE MY FATHER'S MEMORY TO GUILT ME INTO DOING WHAT SHE WANTS.
I'LL HELP HER. AND I WON'T GIVE UP. IT'S WHAT YOU DO FOR FAMILY.
BUT MOTHER'S GOT TO REALIZE, I CAN'T BE CONTROLLED BY HER.
AND THERE ARE BIGGER THINGS GOING ON THAN WHAT SHE WANTS RIGHT NOW.
IT'S UP TO ME TO FIGURE THEM OUT.

I'M MY OWN PERSON.
AND THIS--
--THIS IS MY HOME.
ONE OF TWO, THAT IS.
IF I'M GOING TO LIVE ON BOTH, I'M GOING TO HAVE TO LEARN TO SHOULDER THE PROBLEMS OF TWO WORLDS.
SHOULDN'T BE TOO MUCH OF A PROBLEM, RIGHT?
AFTER ALL, I'M
SUPERGIRL
THIS IS MY LIFE.
END

SUPERGIRL 34 VARIANT COVER
FERNANDO PASARIN AND MATT RYAN
WITH BRAD ANDERSON

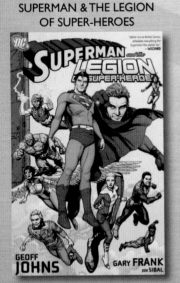